EDUCATION AND COMMU

Other titles in the Cassell Education series

Education and Community

The Politics of Practice

Edited by
Garth Allen and
Ian Martin

CASSELL

Cassell

Villiers House	387 Park Avenue South
41/47 Strand	New York
London WC2N 5JE	NY 10016–8810

© The editors and contributors 1992

First published 1992

British Library Cataloguing-in-Publication Data
A catalogue record for this book is available from the British Library.

ISBN 0–304–32631–3 (hardback)
      0–304–32629–1 (paperback)

This book is dedicated to the memory of Harry Rée

Typeset by Colset Private Limited, Singapore
Printed and bound in Great Britain by Dotesios Ltd., Trowbridge

Contents

The Contributors

Garth Allen is Head of the Department of Social Sciences at the College of St Mark and St John, Plymouth. He has a particular interest in education as social policy and has written extensively on political education. He is co-editor of *Community Education: An Agenda for Educational Reform*, 1987.

Emma Beresford has worked for several years as a Community–School Liaison Teacher in an inner city comprehensive school in Manchester. She is currently conducting comparative research on parental involvement for Manchester LEA and developing independent training and consultancy work.

Sue Charteris is Executive Director (Corporate Resources), Kirklees Metropolitan Council. Her current interests focus on ways of making local government services more effective, responsive and accountable. She was previously Policy Development Co-ordinator in the London Borough of Ealing and has wide experience in community development and equal opportunities work.

David Clark is Senior Lecturer in Community Education at Westhill College, Birmingham. His current interests include action-research on the introduction of community education perspectives in the National Curriculum. He is also a Methodist minister and has published extensively on community education, the sociology of community and theology.

Pam Flynn is Head of the Community Education Service, Newcastle upon Tyne. She has wide-ranging experience in non-formal adult education and action-research in inner city areas. She is co-editor of *You're Learning All the Time: Women, Education and Community Work*, 1986.

Liz Foster is Lecturer in Special Needs employed by Bolton Community Education Service. She has a particular interest in the development of educational responses to the closure of psychiatric hospitals and 'care in the community'. Previously she co-ordinated adult basic education in Prestwich Psychiatric Hospital.

Roger Giles is Vice-Principal of Burleigh Community College, Leicestershire. He has extensive experience in educational administration and local policy development in the Metropolitan Borough of Rochdale. He has also worked in several secondary community schools and in new town community development.

Beth Humphries is Head of the Social Work Department at Manchester Polytechnic. She previously worked at Liverpool and Newcastle Polytechnics after extensive experience in social work in both the voluntary and statutory sectors. She has carried out research on volunteers and women as learners, and has a particular interest in access issues in higher education.

Tony Jeffs teaches in the Department of Applied Social Studies, University of Northumbria at Newcastle, Newcastle upon Tyne. His main interests are in youth work, youth policy, community schools and social policy. He has written extensively in these fields and is co-editor with Mark Smith of *Informal Education*, 1989.

Rennie Johnston is Lecturer in Community Education at Southampton University. Much of his work involves collaboration with LEAs and other agencies in the development and evaluation of responsive community-based adult education. He has participated in a number of action-research projects with unwaged adults and has published several accounts of this work.

Sue Mansfield is Lecturer in Community and Continuing Education at Northern College in Dundee. She has considerable experience in local authority youth work, community education and policy development. Her current research interests are in feminist theory and practice, women's studies and the role of women in the historical development of community-based adult education in Scotland.

Ian Martin is Lecturer in Community Education at Edinburgh University. He previously combined teaching community education and social policy at Chester College of Higher Education with independent research and consultancy work. He is co-editor of *Community Education: An Agenda for Educational Reform*, 1987.

Mark Smith is Research Fellow and Tutor at the Centre for Professional Studies in Informal Education at the YMCA National College, London. He has published extensively in the fields of youth work, informal education and social policy. He edits the *Social Work and Social Welfare Yearbooks* with Pam Carter and Tony Jeffs.

Introduction

In the late 1980s and early 1990s many of those involved in education and social services delivered by local government were left with a recurring sense of being overtaken by events. The intensification of work resulting from the battery of increasingly radical legislative 'reform' left little time for reflection or genuine professional development. In such a sustained climate of crisis management it often seems difficult either to look back or to look forward. This book, however, is an attempt to do both. It brings together accounts by a variety of contributors who have a particular interest in the interface between education, social welfare and the community, how this has changed in recent years and what its prospects are at a time when the values of self-interest threaten to overwhelm those of social solidarity.

In this respect, the book reflects a significant but largely unremarked trend in local education authority policy development both immediately before and after the Education Reform Act of 1988. This focuses on the relationship between local education services and their constituent communities of residence, interest and need. That such local policy is largely ignored in academic commentaries and policy analysis is not surprising. David Hargreaves (1989) notes that academics and researchers tend to locate and address policy issues at macro, national level and to neglect the processes by which they are interpreted and implemented at local and institutional levels. The effects of this are both reductionist and determinist. It leads to an underestimation of the relative autonomy both of local government and institutions as mediating structures and of workers as individuals and groups. As Stephen Ball (1990) argues:

> The point is not that there are no constraints acting upon the form, process and content of education (there are many), but rather that education is not immediately and directly produced by these constraints.

Similarly, there is often a tendency in macro-analysis to blur the distinction between government and state and so to assume that the relationship between policy making and policy implementation is relatively unproblematic. As a consequence, academic commentary and analysis may become locked into a 'discourse of critique' to the exclusion of a 'discourse of possibility' (Aronowitz and Giroux, 1985).

Throughout the 1980s and into the 1990s many local education authorities, mainly but by no means exclusively Labour controlled, issued policy documents on 'community education'. To the extent that it has attracted the critical attention of mainstream academics at all, community education has been regarded with considerable scepticism – sometimes, admittedly, for good reason, as argued in some of the chapters in Part I (Rethinking Ideas) of this book. The recent groundswell of interest in community education, however, has not been primarily an attempt to revive those established patterns of local policy and practice which have their origins, for instance, in the Cambridgeshire village colleges of Henry Morris and the post-war Leicestershire community colleges or the Educational Priority Area and Community Development Project experiments of the late 1960s and 1970s. On the contrary, they are better understood as a strategic response by LEAs to recent and current pressures on local education services. As Steve Baron (1988) convincingly argues on the basis of a careful consideration of historical evidence:

> Community education should be understood as specific interventions into specific contexts and not as an itinerant, rather timeless, educational strategy looking for a home.

Moreover, these pressures, albeit catalysed by the thrust of central government policy and ideology, reflected widely held – if by no means universal – public concerns and anxieties about state education and welfare services. They echoed what has been described as a 'new consensus of disenchantment' with the post-war welfare settlement (Papadakis and Taylor-Gooby, 1987). As far as education in particular is concerned, the key element of this may be summarized as:

– 'legitimation crisis', a general loss of confidence in the efficacy of public sector education, especially in terms of 'standards' and 'discipline';
– 'distribution failure', a widespread acknowledgement of the failure of state intervention to achieve progressive redistribution of social and educational opportunity;
– 'paternalism', a growing sense among many of the worst off that public sector education and welfare services can operate in oppressive and manipulative ways.

'Thatcherite populism', of course, exploited this widespread sense of disillusion. The political ascendancy of the New Right ensured that retrenchment became the common-sense response to fiscal crisis and into this was woven the ideological onslaught on 'dependency'. In the process, some of the key concerns on the traditional community education agenda were seized upon and reversed: what Miriam David (1989) identifies as a 'narrow and particularistic sense of individuality' sought to transform parent–teacher partnership into parent power, communal solidarity into competitive self-interest, equal opportunities into individual choice.

Spurred on by the overt hostility of central government, many LEAs began to construct a defensive local politics of education around the notion of 'community'. Implicit within this was an admission that the consensus of disenchantment was not merely the product of a New Right conspiracy but also a symptom of the failure in significant respects of the social democratic welfare politics of 1960s and 1970s. Explicit within it was an awareness of the far-reaching nature of structural change in and between communities and regions, for example in the form of long-term unemployment, growing social and economic inequality and permanent demographic change. There was, therefore, an increasing recognition of the urgent need for local education policy to address the changing realities of community life.

The most detailed and systematic of the policy statements emerging from this process of internal review and reassessment was issued by the London Borough of Newham in 1985. Significantly, it starts by identifying community education directly with a policy commitment to equal opportunities and proceeds to demonstrate through a detailed analysis of local data the relative underachievement and educational inequality among its own school leavers and members of the wider community. Other LEA documents, if somewhat less self-critical, nevertheless emphasize the failure of education to provide a service which is genuinely accessible, equitably distributed and perceived as relevant to local people's lives. (For other recent examples of local policy statements, see Birmingham City Council Education Department, 1989, Metropolitan Borough of Rochdale, 1989 and Cambridgeshire County Council, 1990.)

At the level of local policy development, therefore, 'community' – whatever its ambivalence in the context of national policy – appears to have a kind of construct validity. It articulates a renewed, commitment to certain core social and educational values which have become increasingly beleaguered in the period of conservative restoration. Fundamentally, these are concerned with reasserting what Herbert Gintis has called the 'prerogatives of persons' over the 'prerogatives of property'. In this sense, the contemporary community education agenda is determinedly subversive. As Part III (Education, Community and Citizenship) of this book demonstrates, it seeks to reconstruct a concept of citizenship that runs directly counter to a pervasive 'privatism' which is rooted in the

> refusal to consider the existence and meaningfulness of any form of collective identity beyond that entailed in belonging to a family system . . . a denial of the idea that power accrues to individuals through the process of conscious and deliberate organization around collective identities.
>
> (Hoggett, 1990)

In more concrete terms, Ward and Taylor's (1986) characterization of community adult education can be generalized to the contemporary movement as a whole. It has three salient features. First, it is informed by an unashamedly egalitarian ethic: it seeks to confront the stark realities of inequality within and between communities and recognizes the danger that education may reinforce rather than redress them. Second, it aims to enable people to engage constructively with the changing realities of life in their communities – in terms, for example, of the educational implications of social polarization, sexual and racial oppression and widespread poverty. Third, it accepts that this requires much more coherent and systematic strategies of intervention, positive action and collaboration at the local level. In particular, it demands policies that reflect the interests, concerns and needs of local people rather than the traditional priorities and procedures of professionals.

The crucial question, of course, is how far this alternative agenda can be put into practice at a time when the context of national policy is so hostile and the autonomy of local government so restricted. This is the key issue addressed by the contributors to Part II (Reworking Practice) of the book.

In addition, there has recently been a revival of interest in the idea of 'community', which is also reflected in some of the papers in this collection. After being in apparent retreat for many years, the concept of community is now in the process of intellectual rehabilitation as recent interest in the 'new social movements' and the 'politics of identity' illustrates. This suggests not that community is antithetical to class but rather that it is precisely what is needed to 'modernize' class analysis, partly by moving the primary focus away from the work-based politics of production to the community-based politics of consumption.

Paul Gilroy (1987), for example, examines the political experience and cultural activity of black people in contemporary British society and argues that his analysis can be generalized to other oppositional social movements centred, for example, on gender, youth and environmental issues:

> For the social movement of blacks in Britain, the context in which . . . [their] demands have been spontaneously articulated has been supplied by a political language premised on notions of community. Though it reflects the concentration of black people, the term refers to far more than mere place or population. It has a moral dimension . . . [it] signifies not just a distinctive political ideology but a particular set of values and norms in everyday life: mutuality, co-operation, identification and symbiosis . . .

What is distinctive about such social movements is precisely their rejection of the 'politricks' of representation (and co-option) and their commitment to an issue- and community-based politics of resistance to subordination.

The subtitle of this book, *The politics of practice*, focuses attention on the ways in which the idea of community as it relates both to local policy development and to popular experience is understood and enacted. Although the current thrust of centrally driven 'reform' is in conflict with the values of progressive redistribution and social justice that are at the heart of the contemporary community education movement, the claim is made here that the realities of practice are not reducible to the intentions of policy: 'the analysis of the noise and heat of reform . . . still begs questions about the implemention and realization of reform' (Ball, 1990).

As Brian Simon (1989) argues, the translation of policy into practice is always a problematic, contested and unpredictable process because of the variability of local circumstance and the capacity of social institutions to resist (often mistaken for inertia). At the same time, the complex dialectics of change may produce 'unintended outcomes – even opposite ones'.

There is already evidence of new communities of interest being forged between teachers, parents and local people in defence of services they value as communal resources. For example, the two secondary schools based at Stantonbury Campus in Milton Keynes responded to Buckinghamshire County Council's decision to reintroduce selective schooling by voting for Grant Maintained status as a way of sustaining their commitment to comprehensive education. This amounted, in effect, to a pre-emptive opting-out of incorporation within a marketized system of education. According to the Chair of Governors of one of the Stantonbury schools (Stantonbury Campus 1990),

> Becoming Grant Maintained has been a wonderful opportunity for parents, governors and teachers to work together for what they believe. Our community has shown that it values our philosophy and practice. We shall build on this strengthened partnership . . . to get the best for our students and community.

The politics of practice is, therefore, about how policy is interpreted on the ground. The stronger the professional element in this process, the less predictable the outcome. But, as the accounts in this book demonstrate, the site of the politics of practice is now changing. As power is simultaneously centralized and devolved and as the strategic role of local government is further eroded, the locus of action moves to community, institutional and individual levels. At the same time, the restructuring of education, health and social service provision creates a new set of roles and relationships within and between the public, private, voluntary and informal sectors of welfare. The chemistry of the new mix is unstable. Again, Simon (1989) emphasizes the open-ended nature of such a process:

> The history of education does not record a straightforward, linear development. On the contrary, there are advances and rebuffs; periods of crisis and periods of resolution of such crises often involving compromises, sometimes defeats or victories. We are living through such a period now. Its outcome is not pre-determined. What actually happens depends on human action. This is the key issue that must be consistently borne in mind.

The contributors to this book are all active agents in the politics of practice. Their varied concerns and spheres of interest reflect the many voices of those who have an interest in the relationship between education, welfare and community life. They do not offer facile or rhetorical answers to the complex problems and challenges that confront them. And yet, although it is in the nature of such accounts that they are grounded within the particularities of specific contexts, they do combine to offer the outlines of an alternative agenda. This is an agenda based on a renewed, if reconstructed, commitment to egalitarianism and social justice, co-operation and partnership, and the democratic control of local services. Ultimately, they all seek to reaffirm Gramsci's injunction to maintain the 'optimism of the will' at a time when it is often difficult to escape a 'pessimism of the intellect'.

REFERENCES

Aronowitz, S. and Giroux, H.A. (1985) *Education under Siege*. London: Routledge & Kegan Paul.

Ball, S.J. (1990) *Politics and Policy Making in Education*. London: Routledge.

Baron, S. (1988) 'Community and the limits of social democracy: scenes from the politics'. In G. Green and S.J. Ball (eds) (1988) *Progress and Inequality in Comprehensive Education*. London: Routledge & Kegan Paul.

Birmingham City Council Education Department (1989) *New Initiative in Community Education and Community Development*.

Cambridgeshire County Council (1990) *Learning Now: The Cambridgeshire Experience of Community Education*.

David, M. (1989) 'Education'. In M. McCarthy (ed.) *The New Politics of Welfare*. London: Macmillan.

Hargreaves, D. (1989) 'Educational policy and educational change: a local perspective'. In A. Hargreaves and D. Reynolds (eds) (1989) *Education Policies: Controversies and Critiques*. Basingstoke: Falmer Press.

Hoggett, P. (1990) *Modernisation, Political Strategy and the Welfare State*. School for Advanced Urban Studies, University of Bristol.

Gilroy, P. (1987) *There Ain't No Black in the Union Jack*. London: Hutchinson.

London Borough of Newham (1985) *Going Community: Community Education in Newham*.

Metropolitan Borough of Rochdale (1989) *Community Education: Learning in Action*.

Papadakis, E. and Taylor-Gooby, P. (1987) *The Private Provision of Public Welfare*. Hemel Hempstead: Wheatsheaf Books.

Simon, B. (1989) 'Education and the social order: the contemporary scene'. In A. Hargreaves and D. Reynolds (eds) *Education Policies: Controversies and Critiques*. Basingstoke: Falmer Press.

Stantonbury Campus (1990) Press release, 14 May.

Ward, K. and Taylor, R. (eds) (1986) *Adult Education and the Working Class*. London: Croom Helm.

Part I

Rethinking Ideas

Chapter 1

Histories of Community Education: A Feminist Critique

Susan Mansfield

Established historical accounts of the development of community education reflect and reinforce the 'patriarchal, paternalistic and sexist attitudes that permeate the movement'. In this timely critique and reconstruction, Sue Mansfield demonstrates the consistent and distinctive contribution of women to the theory and practice of community education. In doing so, she addresses a fundamental deficiency in the conventional wisdom of a movement which has effectively discounted the contribution of women as women. Using the distinction as well as the tensions between 'liberal' and 'liberating' traditions, she shows why a feminist analysis is needed both to rewrite the history of community education and to make sense of a substantial element of contemporary practice. In the process, she indicates how feminists have consistently used their experience of inequality and oppression to make the connections between action and reflection, personal and political, formal and informal, process and product. The chapter draws upon a range of source material which, like the women it is about, demands to be reinstated within the literature of community education.

INTRODUCTION

The process of rewriting history is one which is frequently regarded with suspicion, tainted as it is by association with totalitarian regimes and the assumption that history represents a procession of unchanging and unchallengeable facts. But for many women it has been and continues to be a very positive process. Consciousness-raising groups within the women's movement have been for me and many other women a means by which we have explored our own past and examined the forces which have shaped our lives. As a consequence of the insights so developed, I have effectively rewritten my own personal history and been enabled to challenge the 'facts' which result in the stereotyping of women. In my work as a community educator with women I have seen the same process taking place repeatedly and increasingly. I have begun to wonder if there was also an alternative women's history of community education waiting to be written. If women as individuals tend to be undervalued and marginalized as members of society, was there a similar tendency to undervalue and marginalize the contribution women had made to the development of community education in Britain? Who determines what represents the history of community education and who records it? Carr (1964), in answer to his own question 'What is history?', replies that it is an interaction, a dialogue between not only the past and present but also between the facts and their recorder. He thus argues that history is never pure because it can never be divorced from the values of the historian who wrote it. One consequence of this is that women (especially working-class women) have been written out of history rather than into it (Rowbotham, 1974; Beddoe, 1987), and thereby prevented from understanding their own historical experience and, instead of building on it, have had to rebuild it (Spender, 1983). If all history is a social construct, defined by the attitudes and opinions of those who 'make' (i.e. write) it, we must be especially concerned with the 'historian' when examining the history of the community education movement.

The recorders, analysts and theorists of community education are overwhelmingly male: O'Hagan (1987) in his list of 'standard texts' on community education includes not one woman writer; the Community Education Development Centre (CEDC) in its source packs (1981, 1985) includes fewer than one woman in four among its contributors (and of the eleven women contributors, seven of them are writing on 'family' issues). Reference to almost any edition of *Community Education Network* (published monthly by the CEDC) demonstrates that the continuing public debate is carried out by a predominantly male network. A recent Open University Press reader (edited by four men) includes only two women out of fifteen contributors (Allen *et al.*, 1987). Is it not significant that Dodds *et al.* (1985), in presenting a radical feminist critique of Martin's (1985) typology of community education models, could identity only one key influence from within the movement and were required specifically to acknowledge the influence of 'discounted' unknown women? If the present 'agenda setters' are almost exclusively male, are they the inheritors of an exclusively male tradition? Or is it that women, as in mainstream history, have been written out and that there is a distinctive strand of women's history, traditions and values for the community education movement to discover?

HISTORICAL ANTECEDENTS OF THE COMMUNITY EDUCATION MOVEMENT

Brookfield (1983) identifies two different models of community education practice that have arisen out of two distinct traditions: *the liberal model*, which is based on the assumption that community education can satisfy the needs of all community members at any one time; and *the liberating model*, which is based on an acknowledgement of inequity and chooses to concentrate on differences and disparities rather than cohesion and harmony. With further subdivisions and alternative labels, other writers subscribe to a broadly similar classification and identify broadly similar historical antecedents from which they developed. But what are the values bequeathed to the movement by such varied antecedents as the settlements, early youth work and the various working-class self-education groups?

Toynbee Hall was both the first of the settlements to be founded (in 1884) and, arguably, the most famous, but it was not necessarily typical of the movement as a whole. It is not always clear today that there were two distinct forms of settlement: men's settlements, such as Toynbee Hall and others, for example, associated with boys' public schools; and women's settlements, which included Talbot House, Bermondsey and Blackfriars. Vicinus (1985) has pointed out that the differences between them were striking, not only physically (the men's tended to resemble Oxbridge colleges whereas the women's were more likely to be like ordinary homes) but also in their methods and ideology. Young Oxbridge graduates staying at one of the men's settlements, in return for offering the expertise they had gained through the privileges of class, were laying the foundations of their future careers. The women at their settlements, however, though also drawn from the educated middle classes, emphasized a shared women's world, based on the assumption that women could reach and help each other despite rather than because of class. Whether they did manage to do so is debatable and there are strong arguments that the settlers benefited more than the slum dwellers from the experience. What is not debatable, though, is that it was primarily these women's settlements which were the precursors of modern approaches to compensatory welfare/education programmes. Nevertheless, modern commentators such as Martin and Brookfield do not acknowledge the distinction between the two types.

The paradox at the heart of these women's settlements was that though they represented a very real degree of freedom for the settlers (who hardly conformed to late nineteenth-century stereotypes of the ideal woman as a wife and mother, being invariably single – even if not necessarily by choice), the values they sought to transmit were of a domestic and stereotyping nature. Few were prepared to admit the incongruity of such independent women working to strengthen family ties, domestic skills and the quality of child-rearing among the urban poor (Vicinus, 1985).

The work of the early pioneers of youth work at this time was also based on Victorian middle-class values. The second half of the nineteenth century and the early years of the twentieth century saw an explosive development of organizations for young people (Percival, 1951), but most were concerned with their spiritual and moral well-being rather than the educational aims we associate with the modern youth service. Accompanying these national organizations (e.g. YMCA, YWCA) and frequently associated with the settlements, there had been a rapid growth in the formation of boys' and girls' clubs. By way of an example of the process by which women's history gets lost, it is interesting to note that whereas the National Association of Boys' Clubs has retained both its name and traditions, few present-day youth workers are aware of the history, or the process, by which the National Organisation of Girls' Clubs was gradually transformed through a number of name changes into Youth Clubs UK. The common denominator between all of these early organizations was their desire to inculcate what they saw as the traditional masculine and feminine virtues (e.g. Ferris, 1918; Percival, 1951; Dawes, 1975; Springhall *et al.*, 1983). Emmaline Pethick and Mary Neal were exceptional in believing that their Esperance Club for working girls should provide economic and industrial education as well as leisure activities (Vicinus, 1985).

Before moving on to consider more radical antecedents, it is worth considering the influence of both the mechanics' institutes and the working men's colleges. Like the settlements and youth work, they are also part of the liberal/reformist (as opposed to liberating/radical) tradition. Indeed, Simon (1985) argues that the mechanics' institutes were a response to the radical activity of the late eighteenth- and nineteenth-century self-help educational groups among the working class. But more importantly, they were also part of the developing patriarchal tradition of adult education. The mechanics' institutes were not intended for women, who were excluded from the decision-making processes even when they did gain access. Women were to experience the same situation when the working men's colleges developed subsequently (Thompson, 1983). Thus, although educated middle-class women did (as practitioners) experience the emancipating effects of the settlement movement, the liberal/reformist tradition had little to offer women in general and virtually nothing in particular. Indeed, even the specific contribution of women to the development of the settlements seems, as in youth work, to have been 'written out' of the history of the movement.

What then of the liberating/radical tradition? Johnson (1979) has demonstrated the educational purpose of the nineteenth century working-class political movements such as Chartism and the Owenites as well as the eighteenth-century corresponding clubs. Women were not excluded by the Owenites (Rowbotham, 1974), who adopted a format which would be familiar to many community educators today. At their informal gatherings, for example, a class leader would start the discussion off and participation in the ensuing debate was open to everyone. But the same could not be said of Chartism: by compromising its earlier demand for universal adult suffrage and petitioning instead for universal male suffrage, the Chartists relegated women to a secondary role. For all Johnson's own careful use of language, the message is inescapable: this tradition's definition of 'really useful knowledge' was essentially a male one with women being defined primarily as wives and mothers rather than workers or political activists (Thompson, 1983).

One kind of 'really useful knowledge' for working women at this time would have been a safe, reliable method of contraception. This, in the form of the cervical cap, was made possible by the discovery in 1843 of how to vulcanize rubber and became an important factor in the development of feminist activity among middle-class women (Branca, 1975). Having gained control of one aspect of their lives, it is not surprising that they should want to exert the same control over other aspects. Working-class women, however, owing to ignorance and expense, continued to be defined by the fertility they could not control.

Thus, from a feminist standpoint, the liberal/reformist tradition and the liberating/radical tradition are based on the same patriarchal values that firmly kept women in their place in the home. Such values were at one with those to be found in the burgeoning schooling system. Education was not to be the emancipating process that Josephine Butler hoped it would be for girls educated in the state sector (see Spender, 1987). Whereas, after the 1870 Education Act, boys were to be educated for the needs of industry and to use their franchise responsibly, girls were to be educated to be good wives and mothers to the workforce rather than to be members of it (see Sharpe, 1976; Davin, 1979; Beddoe, 1987).

Does all this mean that women in community education do not have a history or tradition that they can work to and build on? What it does mean is that women must look beyond O'Hagan's 'standard texts' (1987). If they do look beyond conventional community education sources, they will find a rich and varied heritage to call their own.

Women's alternative histories of community education

Just because working-class men in the form of Chartism had turned their backs on the fight for women's suffrage does not mean that working-class women ceased to fight on their own behalf. The popular image of the campaign for women's suffrage is dominated by the suffragette activities of the Women's Social and Political Union (led by the Pankhurst family and with a mainly educated middle-class membership), but from the 1860s onwards, particularly in Lancashire and Cheshire, the fight was carried on by radical working-class suffrage (as distinct from suffragette) groups which were frequently associated with women's trade union activity. Throughout the movement there was a recognition of the need for women not just to achieve the franchise, but to be enfranchised; that is, to be able to use their votes (when achieved) in a committed and responsible way. There thus developed a wide range of educational initiatives within the suffrage movement. These included informal study groups of women who met in each other's homes, such as those of Cissy Foley (a jack frame tenter in a Bolton spinning mill) and her friends, where they discussed not just votes for women but politics and culture (Liddington and Norris, 1978). Others were involved in setting up more formal classes. For example, Ada Nield Chew in a letter to *Common Cause* (the weekly paper of the National Union of Women's Suffrage Societies) recalled how she had some years earlier been part of a class formed to study the economic position of women and how they had later set out to reach married working women with a class on 'Home and Child Study' (Chew, 1982). She was at this time employed by the Women's Trade Union League as a full-time organizer and in this capacity travelled extensively, always accompanied by her young daughter, training and supporting women in their trade union activities.

The suffrage movement's practice of holding large public meetings required women with confidence and public speaking skills to address them. The Actresses' Franchise League set up elocution classes and taught such skills to potential speakers and local leaders in addition to putting on plays and readings itself (Holledge, 1981). The growing involvement of women in late nineteenth-century and early twentieth-century socialism also required them to develop public speaking skills, and the success with which they achieved this is demonstrated by such initiatives as the Clarion Van. Julia Dawson, a prominent member of the International Labour Party and a contributor to the *Clarion* paper, suggested that her readers sponsor a travelling horse-pulled van to spend the summer touring small towns in the north of England 'introducing Socialism'. Thus in June 1896 three women began a thirteen-week programme of public meetings (Chew, 1982).

The socialist Sunday schools were also an important grounding for women. Annie Davison, recalling her Glaswegian childhood, speaks of how each week they had a speaker who talked about the history of the 'common people' rather than kings and queens. She was later to become one of these speakers herself and remained an active socialist all her life. Many others, however, found that marriage resurrected all the old values and that radical socialist men were not necessarily supportive of what they were trying to achieve for themselves. Hannah Mitchell, a rare working-class suffragette, speaks wryly of her own early married life, recalling that though her husband and his male friends spent their Sundays discussing freedom, liberty and suchlike, she spent her Sundays (her only day off from her job) providing them with the Sunday dinner and home-made teas that they expected! Despite being born in 1871 she had only two weeks' formal schooling and her entire education was accomplished within the context of the International Labour Party, the Clarion Movement and the Women's Social and Political Union, for which she was an active public speaker (Mitchell, 1984).

If the suffrage movement was one major educative force in working women's lives, the Women's Co-operative Guild was another. Founded in 1883 by Mrs Acland and Mrs Lawrenson (Llewelyn Davies, 1984), it too was originally based on values which defined women in terms of their domestic roles (Thompson, 1981), but under the influence of Margaret Llewelyn Davies (organizing secretary from 1889 to 1921) it developed into a major campaigning body with a strong democratic structure and an equally strong commitment to women's education. She was responsible for collecting together the writings of the members and, on the urging of Virginia Woolf, had them published. Women wrote not only most graphically about their lives and everyday experiences but also, movingly, about the impact the Guild's activities had on their lives. The real strength of the Guild was that it enabled women to learn directly from their own and each other's experiences both inside and outside the Guild. Further, building on Llewelyn Davies's foundations, it continued to promote training and educational programmes that, through formal classes or the informal social meetings, were never divorced from action but were an integral part of the Guild's activities and structure (Stott, 1973; Spender, 1983).

The tradition of women recognizing that they needed to be fully 'enfranchised' to gain emancipation did not end with the passing of the 1928 Electoral Reform Act (which finally brought universal adult suffrage to Britain). Nor, with the arrival of the Welfare State, did women stop campaigning, and learning in the process, for social justice. There was, however, a need for change and this was recognized. Thus the National Union of Women's Suffrage Societies disbanded itself and took the decision to form Townswomen's Guilds (Stott, 1978) with the specific aim of attracting women who had not previously been involved in the women's movement. The intention was to encourage women to make good use of their vote by providing them with space to meet in order to exchange experiences and skills with a view to widening their interests and building their confidence. Constance Rover has pointed out that the Women Citizens Association had very similar aims, with a strong emphasis on current affairs and discussion of how they affected women (Spender, 1983).

The list could go on of women's organizations that, though not normally associated with community education, do see themselves as having aims that are broadly in line with those most community educators would say they are working to, even though this may not be acknowledged by the community education establishment. Thus, for example, although the Women's Institute movement is popularly characterized (or caricatured) by jam making and flower arranging, it maintains its own residential college with a varied educational and training programme, has a strong national democratic structure and is increasingly adopting a harder campaigning stance on many issues of concern to its members. Perhaps it should not be so lightly dismissed. Similarly, the Pre-school Playgroup Association, by the nature of its structure and method of working with parents (which in the vast majority of cases means mothers), would probably repay closer examination of its process of involvement as opposed to simple examination of its programmes. Feminist community educators are far more likely to draw on their experience of the women's movement to inform their practice than to draw upon any of the traditionally accepted models of community education. Uncomfortable though it may be, the fact remains that from a feminist perspective all these mainstream models are based on histories, traditions and values that are patriarchal in nature.

Consequences of patriarchal heritage for the community education 'movement'

Though it is beyond the scope of this chapter to consider the consequences of patriarchal heritage for the community education 'movement' in great depth, the point must be made that the movement will eventually have to face up to some central contradictions. Women's life patterns tend to be different from those of men but most educational planning is not responsive to this. Although it is far from easy to provide suitable programmes (Hughes and Kennedy, 1985), community educators *must* ensure that their actions and programmes do fit into these patterns if they are to be true to their aims. They must also be prepared to acknowledge that much community education is in reality concerned with the education of women, be it in the form of parent education, family centres, mother and toddler groups, English as a second language or Adult Basic Education. Further, they must recognize that when they set out to identify and meet the 'needs of women', they are often continuing to define them by their relationships to others – as homemakers, mothers and economic dependants. It is not sufficient for practitioners and theorists alike to say that community education should be about partnership and solidarity rather than paternalism or manipulation (Martin, 1987). Nor is it acceptable to argue that the crucial issue in community education is not what a hard-working paternalism will provide for the people (Keeble, 1981) and, therefore, to assume that the movement is safe from accusations of paternalism, when patriarchal, paternalistic and sexist attitudes permeate it, as evidenced both in the 'standard texts' and the received histories of the movement. The language used by many writers often betrays an uncritical acceptance of older values despite the fact that in community education many of the practitioners and most of the participants are women.

I began by arguing that what people choose to record as 'history' tells us as much about them and their values as it does about the past. The currently acknowledged histories of community education, by largely ignoring the role played by women (both past and present), tell us much about the attitudes and values currently held by the movement. For the future, it must face up to the challenge presented by feminist critiques and recognize the inherent contradictions they expose between practice, aims and values. For the present, it could begin by acknowledging the legacy that women and women's organizations have bequeathed it and to recognize the models of good practice that are to be found in the women's movement.

REFERENCES

Allen, G., Bastiani, J., Martin, I. and Richards, K. (1987) *Community Education: An Agenda for Educational Reform*. Milton Keynes: Open University Press.
Beddoe, D. (1987) *Discovering Women's History: A Practical Manual*. London: Pandora.
Branca, P. (1975) *Silent Sisterhood: Middle Class Women in the Victorian Home*. London: Croom Helm.
Brookfield, S. (1983) *Adult Learners, Adult Education and the Community*. Milton Keynes: Open University Press.
Carr, E. H. (1964) *What Is History?* Harmondsworth: Penguin.
Chew, D. N. (ed.) (1982) *Ada Nield Chew: The Life and Writings of a Working Woman*. London: Virago.
Community Education Development Centre (1981) *Outline 1: A Source Pack for Community Education*. Coventry: CEDC.

Community Education Development Centre (1985) *Outlines, Volume 2*. Coventry: CEDC.

Davin, A. (1979) 'Mind that you do as you're told: reading books for Board School Girls, 1870-1902'. *Feminist Review*, **3**.

Dawes, F. (1975) *A Cry from the Streets: The Boys' Club Movement in Britain from the 1850s to the Present Day*. Hove: Wayland Publishers.

Dodds, G., Harrison, D. and Martin I. (1985) 'Community Education: a feminist perspective'. *Journal of Community Education*, December, 19–23.

Ferris, H. J (1918) *Girls' Clubs: Their Organisation and Management*. London: Rent.

Holledge, J. (1981) *Innocent Flowers: Women in the Edwardian Theatre*. London: Virago.

Hughes, M. and Kennedy, M. (1985) *New Futures: Changing Women's Education*. London: Routledge & Kegan Paul.

Johnson, R. (1979) 'Really useful knowledge, radical education and working class culture'. In J. Clarke, C. Critcher and R. Johnson (eds) *Working Class Culture*. London: Hutchinson.

Keeble, R. W. J. (1981) *Community and Education*. Leicester: National Youth Bureau.

Liddington, J. and Norris, J. (1978) *One Hand Tied behind Us*. London: Virago.

Llewelyn Davies, M. (ed.) (1984) *Life As We Have Known It*. London: Virago.

Martin, I. (1985) 'Ideology and practice in community education'. *Community Education Networks*, **5**(2). Coventry: Community Education Development Centre.

Martin, I. (1987) 'Community education: towards a theoretical analysis'. In G. Allen, J. Bastiani, I. Martin and K. Richards (eds) *Community Education: An Agenda for Educational Reform*. Milton Keynes: Open University Press.

Mitchell, G. (ed.) (1984). *The Hard Way Up: The Autobiography of Hannah Mitchell, Suffragette and Rebel*. London: Virago.

O'Hagan, B. (1987) 'Community education in Britain: some myths and their consequences'. In G. Allen, J. Bastiani, I. Martin and K. Richards (eds) *Community Education: An Agenda for Educational Reform*. Milton Keynes: Open University Press.

Percival, A.C. (1951) *Youth Will Be Led: The Story of the Voluntary Youth Organisations*. London: Collins.

Rowbotham, S. (1974) *Hidden from History: Three Hundred Years of Women's Oppression and the Fight against It*. London: Pluto Press.

Sharpe, S. (1976) *Just Like a Girl: How Girls Learn to Be Women*. Harmondsworth: Penguin.

Simon, B. (1985) *Does Education Matter?* London: Lawrence & Wishart.

Spender, D. (1983) *There's Always Been a Women's Movement This Century*. London: Pandora Press, Routledge & Kegan Paul.

Spender, D. (1987) *The Education Papers: Women's Quest for Equality in Britain, 1850–1912*. London: Routledge & Kegan Paul.

Springhall, J., Fraser, B. and Hoare, M. (1983) *Sure and Steadfast: A History of the Boys' Brigade 1883–1983*. London: Collins.

Stott, M. (1973) *Forgetting's No Excuse*. London: Faber & Faber.

Stott, M. (1978) *Organisation Women: The Story of the National Union of Townswomen's Guilds*. London: Heinemann.

Thompson, J. (1981) 'The educational needs of women in the community'. In *Outlines 1: A Source Pack for Community Education*. Coventry: Community Education Development Centre.

Thompson, J.L.C. (1983) *Learning Liberation: Women's Response to Men's Education*. Beckenham: Croom Helm.

Vicinus, M. (1985) *Independent Women: Work and Community for Single Women 1850–1920*. London: Virago.

Chapter 2

The State, Ideology and the Community School Movement

Tony Jeffs

In this chapter Tony Jeffs presents an iconoclastic onslaught on the community school and college movement. He argues that it has always promised much more than it has delivered. Internally managed by charismatic leaders and externally manipulated by the state, the movement as a whole has singularly failed either to humanize schooling or to open up education to new constituencies. This is largely because it has never been informed by a coherent theory of practice and has lacked the intellectual curiosity to develop one. Despite its credibility gap, however, the origins of the movement are rooted in a communitarian ethic and a progressive tradition that run directly counter to the current atomization of education and the values of 'enterprise'. The latter present a direct and perhaps overwhelming challenge to the comprehensive principle in education. If, however, the community school movement can rediscover itself, it could yet provide the focus for an alternative and genuinely popular agenda for social and educational reform. This is its greatest challenge and possibly its last opportunity.

CONSERVATISM OF SCHOOL AND TEACHER PRACTICE

I confess I am not charmed with the ideal of life held out by those who think that the normal state of human beings is that of struggling to get on; that the trampling, crushing, elbowing and treading on each other's heels, which form the existing type of social life, are the most desirable lot of human kind or anything but the disagreeable symptoms of one of the phases of industrial progress.

(John Stuart Mill)

Community schools have been around for a long time, but still they retain an aura of modernity. The first of the Cambridgeshire village colleges is now over sixty years old. Yet when they are considered as a concept, time seems scarcely to have aged them; only the bricks appear to have weathered. There are several reasons for this. One is that the theory of community schools has barely progressed during the intervening years. That embodied in the 1924 Memorandum of Henry Morris might with minimal adaptation serve today as a manifesto for the community school movement. Indeed, as any reading of the bulk of the policy documents produced by local education authorities (LEAs) during the last two decades arguing for community education initiatives and/or community schools shows, while the literary style has deteriorated the loss has in no way been compensated for by improved analysis or theory. Intellectual progress within this area of education has lagged well behind the building programme.

A major factor has been the innate conservatism of so much school and teacher practice. Community schools so often appear radical precisely because they are set beside provision that is in so many respects reactionary and fixed. Small gains such as the encouragement of parents to contribute within the classroom, adults attending courses and community access to facilities are important but they only retain the air of the chic because most schools have so successfully resisted such minimalist changes. Of course, since the 1920s buildings have in the main become airier, brighter and more 'attractive', equipment updated and school students better clothed and fed. Similarly, the curriculum has expanded and the content been reformulated to take account of the expansion in knowledge and the branching of disciplines. But in other respects, Morris would encounter little today that would surprise him. For all the newspeak and managementese that sprinkle the conversation of some teachers the reality is that the administrative structure of most schools may now have a longer tail, but it is still wedded to the same hierarchical principles. Headteacher dominance continues to be the norm with teachers, students and the community overwhelmingly consigned to the administrative sidelines. In six decades the community school movement has done little, if anything, to dent that tradition. Worse, in certain respects the movement has given it an added lustre. As subsequently noted, it has expanded the resources controlled by headteachers in terms of staffing, funds and facilities without seriously extending democratic accountability to colleagues, users or the wider community however defined. Linked to this has been the emergence of the high profile, charismatic community school head. These 'leaders of the people' were not an unfortunate by-product but were central to the community school/college project.

Just as Morris saw the warden as the epicentre of his project, so today. These demigods still dictate the pace of change and possess the power of veto to the extent that 'the centralisation of power and status that heads enjoy is almost unique in British organisations' (Torrington and Weightman, 1988). The same researchers (interestingly, from a management school rather than an education department) comment:

> '[we are] baffled by the universal conviction among everyone we have spoken to about the power of the headteacher, who has organisational dominance to a degree almost unknown in our experience of studying management in a wide range of undertakings . . . [it] was an impediment to improving efficiency.
>
> (Torrington and Weightman, 1988)

Consequently, as Lewis (1985) and Phillips *et al.* (1985) found, significant change within schools can be achieved only with the consent of the headteacher. Since the 1920s headteachers have not displayed, except in a few noteworthy settings, any inclination to slacken the reins of control. Indeed, as the size of the institutions has expanded, the specialization within disciplines become more pronounced and the bureaucracy and hierarchy within schools formalized into 'posts of responsibility', so the distance and isolation of the headteachers have tended to grow. Hiding behind the tasks of administration, secretarial moats and flashing lights on the door, many have only minimal contact with pupils, parents and teachers. They rarely share either the classroom experiences of the teaching staff or their subject expertise. Therefore, managerialism has been increasingly reified into a science to justify high salaries and status.

This importation, designed to bolster an entrenched and inappropriate hierarchy, has been both idiosyncratic and all too often irrational. Inevitably, crude unrefined models from the corporate and industrial spheres have been imported to provide justification and mystification.

Community schools and the rhetoric of community education have shown little propensity to undermine this reality. Indeed, in many respects they have strengthened the processes of centralization both by administrative fiat and the subtle subversion of the language of devolution and autonomy. From the onset community schools have been justified and funded as a mechanism for the centralization of service delivery, the achievement of economies of scale and the more effective monitoring of public expenditure. They have been used as a conduit via which resources for adult education, youth provision, leisure, community development and other services could be integrated within the mainstream, not in the interests of the consumer but of the provider: a means by which accountability upwards could be reinforced and previously diverse activities monitored. Notably those community schools that sought to devolve power have tended to find themselves acutely exposed to diverse pressures that they were unable to handle. Experiments designed to 'democratize' the school structure, such as those initiated at Countesthorpe College and Sutton Centre, have failed to survive in that form. Their history has been not only troubled but also marked by the slow but measured imposition of traditional modes of management (Fletcher *et al.*, 1985).

It remains the case that to date no evidence can be cited, beyond the anecdotal, that they have improved the quality of service delivery. Indeed, it is astounding just how little research has been carried out even though 'pilot' work has indicated the need for it, in particular in relation to adult education and youth work provision (see, for example, Wallis and Mee, 1983; Whiteside, 1984; Shiels, 1985). What does exist indicates that they have achieved little in extending the take-up of adult education or changing the class profile of consumers (Mason, 1978; Wallis, 1983) or even producing among their students more positive attitudes towards either school or post-compulsory education (Bobbe, 1986). In the absence of any other explanation, one is driven to the conclusion that research has been eschewed, not on the grounds of irrelevance, but because it would undermine a pre-ordained policy and the entrenched interests of LEAs and those who currently manage these institutions. Out of self-interest those who control the resources required for effective research appear to have deliberately withheld them. As a consequence, community schools have barely had to justify either their creation or existence. They have been assumed to be of self-evident merit, like the schools upon which they have been grafted; only the minutiae of practice may be questioned, not the institution itself. The need to create a passable theory has been avoided and the literature has remained overwhelmingly acritical and atheoretical, partial and anodyne. The posturings of the self-publicist or charlatan have rarely been challenged, and what passes for policy has amounted to little more than incremental pragmatism.

In a period of growth and expansion the absence of theory and research was barely noticed. Indeed, in the heady round of creating yet more of the same or reconstructing the tired old comprehensive and tripartite school into a spanking new 'community' one, devoting time and energy to theory making and analysis seemed almost irrelevant and other-worldly – a dereliction of duty when the real job was to proselytize the message. Now that the merry-go-round has slowed, it becomes obvious that the failure to pay attention to research, theory and evaluation has been disastrous. When attacked by those who reject the ideological premise of community schools, their erstwhile advocates all too often seem incapable of a coherent response. Lacking a clear grasp of the philosophy that underwrote them as well as a theory of their role and purpose, they seem ill-equipped to resist the pressures of a government determined to refashion schools in the Thatcherite image. Gone are the fair-weather converts and opportunists of yester-year, they have already deserted the bandwagon to become born-again new vocation-alists and market-led providers rather than educationalists. Of course few, one suspects, seriously believed the rhetoric of community power or autonomy in the first place. Encountering little that is either threatening or philosophically uncomfortable about the new orthodoxy, they wholeheartedly embrace it. For after all, it is a theory, tradition and ideology which are a reflection of and justification for the very forms of manage-ment and structure they never actually jettisoned.

LEADERSHIP AND THE COMMUNITY SCHOOL

Concentrating and integrating provision within school settings has meant, as already noted, the endorsement of a hierarchical management structure. No evidence exists that community schools have in any way undermined the resilience of this tradition. Indeed, alternative pluralist, socialist or libertarian models have either been excluded from consideration or undermined, and in some cases dismantled, as a consequence of com-munity school expansion. For example, the history of community schools has lent heavily on a charismatic tradition. This is largely recounted by reference to a series of great chief officers and heads who by dint of Herculean energy, force of intellect or, more usually, the power of their personality, wrought change and regeneration within authorities or schools (see, for example, Ree, 1973; Jones, 1987, 1988). The message has always been to learn by imitation. This was partly because their success appeared to flow from character rather than theory but also because there was little besides an oral tradition within the history of community schools. However, apart from a role model and the opportunity to follow in the footsteps of greatness, it also offered heads the promise of higher income, higher status and higher profile. *In extremis* it fed a mega-lomania wherein it became possible, according to the Morris model of leadership, not only for the 'new' head to shape the character of the young within the school but also fashion the community outside it. Either way, it presented an opportunity for sustaining middle-class, white and overwhelmingly patriarchal community leadership.

For Morris, the problem that had presented itself was clear. A vacuum of leadership was apparent in rural England during the 1920s. Battered and bruised by falling land and agricultural prices, the old 'squirearchy' seemed on the verge of extinction. Owner-ship was transferring to absentee landlords in the form of large insurance or conglomer-ate companies. These, in the best traditions of finance and industrial capital, could be expected to exhibit minimal concern for the moral, social and economic welfare of those living on or adjacent to the land they possessed. *Noblesse oblige* did not figure on their balance sheet, and the only tone they might be expected to set was one sympathetic to exploitation and indifferent to the unproductive. Linked to the unremitting decline in the influence of the Church as a unifying force within rural communities was a conse-quent erosion of its ability to set the 'moral' tone. The solution was to fabricate around and within the one remaining universal institution – the school – a new site for leader-ship and cohesion; to reconstruct the headteacher into a warden not only of the school but of the community itself.

In the post-war period de-urbanization gathered pace and housing policy deftly sepa-rated the classes and, to an extent, black and white into their respective ghettos. Decamping to their suburbs and semi-rural retreats, a car journey away, the indigenous white middle class left behind them an economic rump. Characterized as constituting at best structureless communities, or at worst an *ad hoc* accumulation of the socially deprived and pathologically inadequate, these localities required more than monitoring. They needed leadership. Adrift at the margins of society, volatile and unsophisticated enough to fall prey to the blandishments of unscrupulous political demagogues, the working class, both white and black, could not be left well alone any longer. If those who extracted the wealth from the inner urban areas or who 'employed' the occupants of the new council estates clustered on their fringes were not willing to live among or even adjacent to them, then the tasks of social management, moral guidance and 'setting an example' had to be subcontracted to paid agents.

For educationalists, and a growing number of others, the community school offered a solution. Even in the suburbs, where the social workers, health visitors and teachers located themselves, community schools proved attractive. There they held out a promise that a community spirit might be constructed despite the absence of any communality apart from a shared spatial locality. Turning dormitory estates and commuter villages into communities was, of course, a far more attractive undertaking than any on offer elsewhere. At least both providers and consumers in those settings shared a common class or racial background and ethos. Where aspirations and values dovetailed, doing *with* rather than doing *for* was on the agenda. Elsewhere, however foolish, naive and preposterous the vision and concept of the community school might be, it was neverthe-less sustained. Enormous effort and commitment on the part of practitioners selflessly willing to work themselves into the ground in order to give community schools meaning kept it alive in some areas; in others an often limitless capacity for self-delusion sufficed; elsewhere the absence of an alternative meant all parties agreed to avoid asking the awkward questions that would expose it for the sham it all too often amounted to.

If the administrative structures of community schools are barely at variance with those found elsewhere, so with pupil–teacher and pupil–school relationships. In most schools (community or otherwise) these are locked into a pattern which in its fundamen-tals was securely entrenched in the public sector by the turn of the century. Apart from the abolition of physical punishment, long resisted by teachers and forced on a recalcitrant government by the European Court, the scale of change has been far less than is often imagined. Pupil rights and involvement in the decision-making process remain so severely curtailed as to be almost non-existent. Schools remain profoundly anti-democratic in form and content. Given the minimal stake in terms of control, perhaps it is not surprising that in most cases neither parental nor pupil loyalty to secondary schools has markedly grown (Ainley, 1988; Meighan, 1981). The anti-intellectualism of so many teachers, linked to anti-working-class attitudes and the politi-cal and educational conservatism so widespread within the profession, have combined to ensure that the wish of Morris that our schools be 're-made' has not come to pass. Certain community schools have, in a limited number of localities, humanized elements of the secondary school system. In the primary sector a number have set the pace regarding greater parental involvement (Rennie, 1985). In both sectors some barriers have been removed that previously separated schools from the wider community and access to facilities has improved. Such achievements should not be denigrated, nor the sacrifices of individuals overlooked, but neither should they be over-estimated. The depth of opposition that schools which have sought to transcend the safe and the predictable have encountered is indicative of the resistance both within and without education to the progressive and liberal. In seeking to calibrate the achievements of community schools it is, therefore, essential to acknowledge the over-arching success of those who have fought a rearguard action to keep British schools tied to an unyieldingly anti-democratic and isolationist tradition.

Although the first two village colleges pre-dated the 1944 Education Act, not too much should be read into this. They were clearly prototypes that might have remained little more than fondly recalled educational Brabazons but for the gradual emergence of comprehensive schools and what one text refers to as the 'settlement of the 1960s' (CCCS, 1981). Morris was certainly in advance of his times as a social democrat and collectivist who, like the more influential Tawney, was obliged to await the post-war settlement before his vision could take shape beyond Cambridgeshire. Philosophically, Morris was a product of the British idealist tradition of T. H. Green and Bosanquet with its belief in fellowship, the brotherhood of man and communitarianism (see Gordon and White, 1979). It was this tradition that provided the impetus for the settlement movement, the origins of British community work and, not least through its influence upon Dewey, contributed to the development of progressivism in British education (Jones, 1983).

The relationship between the community school movement and the rise of the comprehensives is a complex one. It was and is possible, to an extent, to have one without the other. Morris proved that to be the case. However, it was the determination of Stewart Mason to create an integrated network of community schools in Leicestershire which produced the first truly comprehensive secondary system (Jones, 1988). Subsequently they have come to be viewed as two sides of the same coin. Initially, community schools acted as a precursor and justification for comprehensive reform, but subsequently the roles have been reversed. The community idea has been envisaged as a means of rescuing under-achieving secondary and primary schools alike, a way of protecting them from criticism, of attracting wider support and affiliation, in some cases becoming reduced to a PR exercise to lift a flagging image. By the mid-1970s the comprehensive system was under serious and sustained attack. Irrespective of the justification for the denigration heaped upon such schools, it has to be recognized that a retreat began during that period which continues unabated today. City Technology Colleges, the National Curriculum, localized pay bargaining for teachers, parental choice and the right of schools to opt out of LEA control all signal major defeats and to varying degrees, unless repealed in the near future, the end for the foreseeable future of the comprehensive system created during the post-war period.

THE BAKER ACT

Appearances can be misleading. It is all too easy to be contemptuous of both the 1988 Education Reform Act (ERA) and its predecessor, the 1986 Education Act. Both have the air about them of shallow thinking and 'back of envelope planning'. Both are the products of administrative arrogance and skimped consultation. Those who constructed them showed complete indifference for the views of the public, pundits, practitioners and experts alike. Indeed, they were constructed according to a timetable that deliberately made consultation, analysis and reflection impossible. Even the totally inadequate safeguards of the parliamentary system were reduced to a shambles and farce with key elements pushed through without anything more than a cursory examination by legislators (Armstrong, 1988). After two decades in which research material and theoretical writings on education proliferated as never before, the legislation that has emerged appears to be the product of the worst sort of Babbitt mentality. A nation of shop-keepers has perhaps at last secured the promise of the education system it deserves. Possibly no greater indictment of the past failings of the British education system can be cited than that such a crude restructuring should provoke only a minimal public outcry. Over-arching indifference to matters of educational policy is the price that those who care must pay for the grotesque failings of generations of colleagues for whom education meant little besides a pay packet, long holidays, middle-class life-style and an easy ride in the classroom.

The Baker Act signals a break with the past even more profound than either the Balfour (1902) or the Butler (1944) Act. Things will never be the same again: the imposition of a centrally determined National Curriculum; the introduction of standardized testing; the weakening of the influence of the teaching profession; the marginalization of teacher unions and abandonment of Burnham; the energetic encouragement of schools to opt out of LEA control and choose between the alternatives of central government funding and the collecting box and corporate begging bowl; the strengthening of the powers of police and, above all, business interest to influence the ethos and management of schools; the creation of a free market among schools to encourage the survival of the most ruthless and the elimination of co-operation; the ending of academic tenure and the creation of new funding bodies for higher education to ensure that universities and polytechnics meet national needs as defined by central government. All these make awesome reading. For those raised on a staple diet of milk-and-water radicalism, apologetic reformism or consensual deference, it is both unpalatable and an object lesson in how to integrate ideological objectives with educational practice and policy. Certainly, after the 1988 Act there can be no going back. Henceforth all attempts to create a more liberatory educational practice, better schools or whatever else may enter the agenda will have to be undertaken within a context dominated by that Act and the enterprise it represents.

The speed with which the Baker Act moved from ministerial hint to bill to law took most parties by surprise. Indeed, if the pace had not disorientated the actual and potential opposition, the careful planning of the Cabinet would have been wasted. Democratic forces and organizations take time to muster their strength. Citizens, as opposed to the bureaucrat and satrap, have to find gaps in a largely predetermined timetable structured around work and home responsibilities to assess proposals and create the space to formulate an intervention. Deny them time and you effectively deny them a role and voice in decision making. As intended, that is precisely what happened. The pluralist democratic process was short-circuited, not because the reforms could not wait upon it, but because the Conservative government and its allies held both the process and those desirous of contributing to the debate in contempt. The gestation period of the Act gave the lie to the claims of its supporters that it was designed to heighten public involvement in education and democratize the school system. If that had been the aim, then it takes only a few moments' reflection to conceive of a fraction of the creative and imaginative ways in which the instigation of 'reforms' might have provided the impetus and backcloth for a genuine and far-ranging public debate about educational policy and practice. Such a debate might have possessed the capacity to produce alternatives rather than allowing time only for negative responses to a given government agenda.

The haste can only be explained by looking beyond the narrowly educational purpose of the legislation to the deeper social engineering project which determined its content and ethos. The timing and thrust as well as the content were, as Simon (1988) argues, enmeshed within a strategy designed to ensure the re-election of a Conservative government for a fourth term, thereby enabling it to achieve the 'elimination of socialism' as a vibrant political current within British politics. Consequently, any educational concerns that conflicted with this over-arching purpose had to be relegated to a supporting role. State schools, like local authority housing, are perceived as potential or actual breeding grounds for alternative cultures and, worse, socialism.

The quasi-independence of LEAs and the relative autonomy of teachers in the classroom both provide opportunities for oppositional practice. The former are legitimized by local democracy and the latter by recourse to professional expertise. If the hegemonic dominance of an enterprise ideology and the 'common sense' of the New Right are to secure an unassailable intellectual and political position, both pose a threat, actual or potential, which has to be neutralized. Therefore LEAs are to be weakened and eventually made redundant not on the grounds that they are inefficient or anti-democratic but because they are or might be legitimately controlled by socialists, and used by the 'enemies within' as a conduit for the dissemination of oppositional ideas. Like the GLC and Metropolitan Councils before them, LEAs are doomed not because they are incompetent or unpopular but precisely because they have the capacity to challenge the unbridled power of central government and its current paymasters.

Such is the confidence of the Conservative Party in its ability to sustain indefinite supremacy via the manipulation of the electoral process and the management of news, media and public opinion that it is willing to centralize control of education in the hands of a Secretary of State on the basis of a model previously in partial operation in Northern Ireland. Such centralization would have been unthinkable a decade ago – partly because it was then politically expedient to sustain the myth of pluralist consensus but also for fear those powers once created could fall into the hands of political opponents. Now it is a gamble the Conservatives are willing to take, confident of success, in order to inflict a major defeat upon a weakened opposition and achieve the commodification of the school system. The values, morality and thought processes of the marketplace are to be forcibly injected into all things educational, from the humblest Wendy House to the newest of new computer laboratories.

COMMUNITY SCHOOLS AND THE 1988 ACT

The Baker Act is not simply a crude frontal assault. It is subtle enough to exploit public anxieties regarding educational standards and, where open doors exist, has sensibly opted to push against them. It expropriates the rhetoric of 'parent power' while busily centralizing control in the hands of Whitehall. It offers the chimera of financial auton- omy while placing it in a strait-jacket of diminishing resources which ensures that schools lack a genuine capacity for innovation and independent action – apart from the dubious power to create ever more imaginative ways to exploit young people, parents and others for the purposes of raising income, not for the frills, but to meet statutory duties. In this and other ways it steals much of the language and rhetoric of community education and the community school movement. However, nobody should be under any illusions that either it or the ideology that inspired it share a similar vision. The commu- nity school movement, as already noted, was the product of a philosophical tradition that gained its strength and momentum during the nineteenth and early twentieth centuries from widespread revulsion and reaction against the same utilitarian and indi- vidualistic beliefs that dominate the thinking of the politicians and educationalists who shaped the 1988 Act. The community school movement, whatever its failings, was an attempt to provide an alternative to crude individualism and the domination of the profit motive, to distribute resources both financial and cultural according to criteria of need rather than income and wealth, a mechanism whereby education might be made available to all. In doing so it sought to 'do away with the insulated school [and] asso- ciate with education all those activities which go to make a full life – art, literature, music, recreation, festivals, local government, politics' (Morris, 1926). Service to the community was to be placed above individual gain as the motivating agent for both the educator and the student. It was a tradition which, as George and Wilding (1985) note, demanded of its affiliates 'cooperation rather than competition, an emphasis on duties rather than rights, on the good of the community rather than on the wants of the individual, on altruism rather than selfishness'. To read anything else into the writings of Morris and those who followed him is to construct a parody of their ideas.

Not only is it crucial to rediscover the ideas that inspired the community school movement and reinterpret them, it is also essential honestly to confront the ideology that produced the ERA. To do so obliges one to acknowledge without illusions that it is inspired by a determination to destroy not only the comprehensive system but also the ideas that shaped the community school movement. Therefore, to secure a compromise between the two would require a rejection of the principles upon which the latter is founded. Swain (1989) may be able to argue from a dictionary definition that 'enter- prise' is a neutral concept wholly compatible with community education's concern with 'life-long learning which is accessible, open, person-centred, community-focused, experiential and needs related and leads to action of mutual benefit to individuals, groups and communities'; by 'empowering' the learner it shares a common heritage with enterprise development processes which, magically, 'also focus upon person-centred, action-orientated learning leads to change'. The implication of such verbiage is that community education can embrace or at least benefit from the so-called enterprise culture. Such double-think is only possible if first one chooses to ignore the essential truth that community education must place at the heart of the project such concepts as fellowship and community, which demand the curtailment and control of self-interest by all parties. It is not person-centred but community-centred because it assumes 'that children cannot grow naturally in isolation from one another, that membership of the community and neighbourhood is central to achieving a fully human condition'

(Barker, 1986). Secondly, it also means that one must not refuse to examine what 'enterprise' has come to mean in the present political context.

Today 'enterprise' has been translated into a euphemism for individual self-interest and the heightened exploitation of others. Enterprise means schools competing for resources and pupils rather than co-operating. It is a system designed to force schools in a period of falling rolls to enter into a free-for-all in which some, by the very logic of numbers, must be driven to the wall. In this way an ERA community school, situated in a comfortable middle-class suburb in the North East, can boast in its advertising brochure that it attracts 20 per cent of its pupils from the catchment area of neighbouring schools in another LEA. In other words, it is ensuring the eventual closure of the school in a nearby working-class community by poaching pupils whose parents have the resources to transport their children across the border. The logical outcome of this is the impoverishment of the educational opportunities of those unable or unwilling to travel, eventually depriving an already underprivileged locality of its school and all the resources that go with it – without, it should be added, having any intention of compensating those people for their loss. In practical terms, this is what enterprise in education means: 'making the good of each depend upon evil to others, making all who have anything to gain or lose live as in the midst of enemies' (Mill, 1851). Intellectually it is about ensuring at all costs the domination of the business ethic within schools, excluding from that domain notions of shared needs and co-operation. By creating competition whereby school is set against school, teacher against teacher and pupil against pupil, it seeks to teach young people such an ethic by lived example, to produce among parents a naked disregard for the needs of other pupils and an unhealthy obsession with the interests of their own offspring. Schools that embrace – let along glory – in this ethic can remain community schools in name only.

Harvey (1990) argues that the ERA and similar measures mean we have probably come to the 'end of the line . . . in community and adult education'. He may be correct, although I think not. Those community schools which have genuinely sunk roots in their locality will survive as alternatives to the dominant model. But for how long, given the odds against them and the determination of schools around them to see them fail? Such schools will need all the support they can get if we are to have anything left on which to build a national community school movement in the future. A number will have to opt out to survive; others may even have to go independent. Elsewhere it will be essential to develop alternative educational programmes capable of attracting support and of inspiring a new generation of educationalists.

In the past the community school movement captured buildings rather than minds. As the events of the last decade have shown, the former are easily lost if the latter are not secured. This means we must, above all, construct a better theory to guide us and a better vision to inspire. Henry Morris operated in a hostile climate and those who still wish to be associated with that tradition will have to learn to do likewise – and fast. Progressive ideas are not in vogue in contemporary educational circles. Those who hold such ideas will have to learn how to survive unpopularity emanating from both colleagues and employers. The easy route to reform, if ever there was one, has for the time being been closed. If Henry Morris provides one model to follow, perhaps in the current climate Kim Philby offers another.

REFERENCES

Ainley, P. (1988) *From School to YTS: Education and Training in England and Wales 1944-1987*. Milton Keynes: Open University Press.

Armstrong, H. (1988) 'Women and children first'. *Times Educational Supplement*, (April), 8.

Barker, B. (1986) *Rescuing the Comprehensive Experience*. Milton Keynes: Open University Press.

Bobbe, B. (1986) 'A comparison of pupils' attitudes towards education and future orientation to learning in community and non-designated schools'. Unpublished M.Ed. thesis. Nottingham University.

CCCS (1981) *Unpopular Education: Schooling and Social Democracy in England since 1944*. London: Hutchinson.

Fletcher, C., Caron, M. and Williams, W. (1985) *Schools on Trial*. Milton Keynes: Open University Press.

George, V. and Wilding, P. (1985) *Ideology and Social Welfare*. London: Routledge & Kegan Paul.

Gordon, P. and White, J. (1979) *Philosophers as Educational Reformers: The Influence of Idealism on British Educational Thought and Practice*. London: Routledge & Kegan Paul.

Harvey, B. (1990) 'The redundancy of community education?' *Community Education Network*, **10** (1), 2.

Jones, D. (1987) 'Planning for progressivism: the changing primary school in the Leicestershire authority during the Mason era, 1947-71'. In R. Lowe (ed.) *The Changing Primary School*. Brighton: Falmer.

Jones, D. (1988) *Stewart Mason: The Art of Education*. London: Lawrence & Wishart.

Jones, K. (1983) *Beyond Progressive Education*. London: Macmillan.

Lewis, J. (1985) 'The theoretical underpinning of school change strategies'. In D. Reynolds (ed.) *Studying School Effectiveness*. Brighton: Falmer Press.

Mason, T. (1978) 'Residential succession, community facilities and urban renewal in Cheetham Hill, Manchester'. *New Community*, **10** (3), 364-72.

Meighan, R. (1981) *A Sociology of Education*. New York: Rinehart & Winston.

Mill, J.S. (1851) 'Newman's political economy'. *Westminster Review*, **56** (October), 440-6.

Morris, H. (1926) 'Institutionalism and freedom in education'. *New Ideals Quarterly*, **2** (1) (March). Reprinted in H. Ree (ed.) (1984) *The Henry Morris Collection*. Cambridge: Cambridge University Press, pp. 34-43.

Phillips, D., Davie, R. and Callely, E. (1985) 'Pathways to institutional development'. In D. Reynolds (ed.) *Studying School Effectiveness*. Brighton: Falmer Press.

Ree, H. (1973) *Educator Extraordinary: The Life and Achievements of Henry Morris*. London: Longman.

Rennie, J. (ed.) (1985) *British Community Primary Schools*. Lewes: Falmer Press.

Shiels, F. (1985) 'School-based youth work'. Unpublished report. Leicester: National Youth Bureau.

Simon, B. (1988) *Bending the Rules: The Baker 'Reform' of Education*. London: Lawrence & Wishart.

Swain, G. (1989) 'Enterprise development in community education'. *Community Education Network*, **9** (11), 2.

Torrington, D. and Weightman, J. (1988) *The Management and Organization of Secondary Schools*. Manchester: University of Manchester Institute of Science and Technology.

Wallis, J. (1983) 'Community schools: theory and practice'. Unpublished Ph.D. thesis. University of Nottingham.

Wallis, J. and Mee, G. (1983) *Community Schools: Claims and Performance*. Nottingham: Department of Adult Education, University of Nottingham.

Whiteside, T. (1984) 'Youth and community education'. Mimeo, Leicester University School of Education.

Chapter 3

Community Education: LEAs and the Dilemmas of Possessive Individualism

Ian S. Martin

There is a strong and varied tradition of LEA policy development in community education. This is seriously threatened by the current restructuring of local government. In particular, the marketization of education subverts the strategic role of LEAs in planning policy in coherent and equitable ways. Ian Martin suggests that community education as a rationale for local education policy stands for a set of values which are in direct contradiction to those which now inform national education policy. It is important that advocates of community education understand this and confront the dilemmas it poses for their own practice. In the vacuum left by the likely demise of local government as we know it, the challenge to community educators is to find new ways of working together and developing strategic responses to change which are consistent with the values they espouse.

THE HEGEMONIC PROJECT

Faced with the urgent realities of institutional change – not to mention professional survival – it is all too easy to lose sight of the wider ideological thrust of policy. The purpose of this chapter is to locate the current restructuring of education and, in particular, its implications for local community education policy within this context. Some of the key concerns raised in the Introduction to this book are developed in order to provide a background to the accounts of the politics of practice which follow in Part II of the text. It should be emphasized that the scope of this discussion is restricted to a consideration of LEA community education policy development in England and Wales. The argument presented here is that although constraints on local government may well generate new opportunities within, for example, the private, voluntary and informal sectors, these cannot be regarded as an adequate substitute for democratically controlled and accountable public policy at the local level.

By the late 1980s the distinctive achievement of Thatcherism – that peculiar blend of conviction politics, populism and pragmatism – was ideological and hegemonic rather than structural and institutional. Only when the ideological groundwork had been systematically prepared could the major social policy 'reform' offensives of the third and fourth terms of Conservative government be launched and consolidated. In its attempt to reconstruct civic culture, the appeal of the New Right was not so much to Victorian values as to those of possessive individualism. In his seminal reinterpretation of the development of English political thought in the seventeenth century, *The Political Theory of Possessive Individualism*, C.B. MacPherson (1962) characterizes possessive individualism in the following terms:

> The human essence is freedom from dependence on the will of others, and freedom is a function of possession. Society becomes a lot of free and equal individuals related to each other as proprietors of their own capacities and of what they have acquired by their exercise. Society consists of relations of exchange between proprietors. Political society becomes a calculated device for the protection of this property and for the maintenance of an orderly relation of exchange.

Throughout the 1980s the hegemonic project of the New Right, modelled on the values of possessive individualism, aimed to effect a radical remoralization of society. As Stephen Ball (1990) argues, 'the role of the New Right, as well as its direct impact on policy in some areas, has been discursive . . . it has facilitated a discursive reworking of the parameters of political possibility and acceptability'.

What changed most radically during the decade of Thatcherism was not so much the infrastructure of the welfare state as the way we were encouraged to think about it. In short, it became acceptable, even respectable, to regard the publicly financed institutions of education, health and welfare as a national liability rather than a national asset – an unwanted and unnatural restraint upon the autonomous activity of free and consenting possessive individualists. By the end of the decade, New Right rhetoric had sought to transform the state as an agent of publicly financed education and welfare from a beast of burden into a beast of prey.

In working out a politics of practice for the 1990s and beyond, it is important to consider where the hegemonic project of the new conservatism has left the LEA sector of community education.

EDUCATION AND THE COMMUNITY

The claim that Henry Morris is the only true begetter of the community education movement has never seemed very convincing. However, his influence remains crucial and still provides a touchstone for gauging its prospects as a rationale for local education policy development. One aspect of Morris's vision and struggle was that he was an ardent and determined advocate of state action to extend educational opportunity. This fact is often neglected because his work tends to be taken out of historical context. His village colleges were essentially about creating a new kind and quality of public education service for local communities in rural Cambridgeshire, especially young people and adults.

This core commitment has remained at the heart of local authority policy development in community education, which is fundamentally about mediating the relationship between lifelong learning and the focus of everyday life in communities. The term 'community education' remains elusive, partly and precisely because its frame of reference is constantly changing and subject to interpretation by many different interests. But the key point is that 'community' is primarily an evaluative, and only secondarily a descriptive, concept. As such, it implies that the social reality to which education must respond constitutes a plurality of interests, needs and aspirations. The process of community education is essentially, as Morris understood, a political process in which the collective dimensions of people's experience and expectations are articulated and reconciled educationally.

As such, community education should be the educational antithesis of what, to paraphrase David Jenkins (Jenkins and Jenkins, 1991), could be called 'the politics of the idiot':

> Originally what was 'common' or 'koinos' went with public duties and opportunities as a citizen, while what was private or 'idios' went with one's own private affairs . . . Now people who stayed out of things also became ignorant of them and incompetent at them . . . Thus as time and usage went on 'idiotikos' went from being a private citizen to being an 'idiot'. That is to say 'idiotic' – incompetently shut up in one's private, limited ways. In short, to be so private and concerned with what is one's own is simply to be an idiot.

Given the struggle between the advocates of voluntary and statutory provision in the 1920s and 1930s (see Baron, 1989), it is perhaps easier to understand the combination of radical ideas and paternalistic action that characterized Henry Morris's work. He was well ahead of his time in many ways. A serious state commitment to secondary education as a public service, eloquently demanded in Tawney's *Secondary Education for All* in 1922, had to await the 1944 Butler Act and, years later, the policy commitment to comprehensive schooling.

Throughout most of the post-war period LEA community education, in both its universalistic and reformist guises, reflected the fragile yet workable social-democratic consensus of 'Butskellism'. This, itself the product of the compromise and accommodation, represented a particular kind of balance between individual and collective interests. Whatever its flaws – and it was a pretty tenuous and expedient affair at times – this consensus was based on a tacit endorsement of state action as a means, among other things, of mitigating the tensions between egoism and altruism, individualism and collectivism, that are inherent in all social policy development. In this sense, part of the purpose of social policy throughout the greater part of the post-war period was precisely to engineer a publicly defensible balance between demand and need, individual self-interest and the good of the wider community.

Despite inevitable stresses and strains, this precarious consensus lasted into the 1970s. Its first serious challenge came with the oil crisis of 1973–4. Shortly afterwards, during the period of the Callaghan government, the retreat started. In this respect, the dynamics of Thatcherism were as much about continuity as change. However, it added its own ideological offensive against the 'nanny state' and the 'dependency culture' to the previous administration's policy of pragmatic retrenchment.

EDUCATION AND THE MARKET

The argument is, therefore, that the Thatcher decade witnessed the initiation and consolidation of the New Right hegemonic project. This was essentially about changing – or trying to change – the way we think about the relationship between the individual and society, the market and the state, self-interest and collective (or 'community') interests. In effect, it was an attempt to legitimize possessive individualism as the moral basis of social action, the idea being that the 'invisible hand' of the market would eventually convert aggregated self-interest into the interests of all. 'Internal markets' in education and health and the 'commodification' of their 'products' are simply tangible expressions of the new hegemony.

It must be emphasized, however, that the market is by no means a neutral mechanism for allocating public goods. As Ruth Jonathan (1990) points out, when the rhetoric becomes reality, the results are invariably regressive:

> What is sold as a loosening of the structure is in fact a *change* in the structure and what results is not an increase in individual freedom, but a *redistribution* of freedoms and opportunities amongst groups of individuals and a redrawing of the parameters of social choice itself.

Part of the logic of market competition in education is the exclusion of the 'bad risk' as institutions vie for custom. The ultimate outcome is likely to be a restratification of the education system and the residualization of particular parts of it in particular areas. The rationale of policy is transformed from equality of opportunity into 'fitness':

> Thatcherism is very much in favour of selectiveness, of allowing the natural difference between people to grow, both as a reward to the talented and successful, the intellectually and morally deserving, and as a spur to the less well-endowed, successful or responsible, to make the most of what they have. This spur is signally absent from a universalistic, social democratic Welfare State.
>
> (Dale, 1989)

PROSPECTS FOR THE FUTURE

Where does this leave the local authority sector of community education? Stranded – a forlorn and anachronistic echo of a discredited era of collectivism? If it is to survive, for the time being it must certainly do so in a cold and hostile climate.

And yet the 1980s and early 1990s also witnessed the emergence of alternative educational agendas at the local level. In particular, as noted in the Introduction, it is significant that throughout this period there was a substantial and distinctive ground-swell of local authority interest in community education – now reinterpreted as a strategy of defence and resistance, or at least containment. But, of course, it is precisely those authorities with a commitment to education as a comprehensive public service that are now most vulnerable. They are among the predictable – and, no doubt, intended – victims of 'the decentralization of operations and the centralization of command' (Hoggett, 1990) that characterizes the current restructuring process.

The emasculation of local government poses critical dilemmas for public sector community education which, given the heterogeneous and unequal nature of communities, should be primarily about strategic planning and intervention. The intention seems to be to replace LEAs, as mediating structures between individuals, communities and the state, with quasi-markets in education which will be controlled by parents as 'consumers', internally regulated by competition for 'customers' and driven by the values of 'enterprise'.

On the other hand, both the internal and the distributive effects of such quasi-markets are difficult to anticipate. As several commentators have argued (e.g. Le Grand, 1990; Moore, 1991), the introduction of the market mechanism in the provision of publicly funded services has the potential to stimulate both 'exit' and 'voice' options: people may vote with their feet and take their custom elsewhere or they may stay put and mobilize internally for change or, indeed, for continuity.

One possible outcome of current educational 'reform' is certainly survival of the fittest and the gradual residualization of the LEA sector of education. If this happens, two perverse mutations of community education may evolve. One model, reflecting the neo-liberal elements of New Right ideology, is that of entrepreneurial 'post-Fordist' schools and colleges selectively hijacking the rhetoric of community education as a public relations exercise so as to ensure their own survival – and to hell with the rest! Individual governing bodies are likely to have little interest in strategic issues of redistribution and equity when their backs are against the wall. As already noted, historically the role of the state (in its benign guise) has been partly to minimize such conflicts of interest. On the other hand, as John Quicke (1988) suggests, there is also scope for an alternative neo-conservative version in which community education is about education for and within 'natural' communities of ability and status in an ordered and hierarchical social structure.

This seems to present a bleak scenario indeed for community education as a rationale for LEA policy development – although, ironically, at a micro level some institutions will begin to practise selectively (for example, in relation to parents in particular) what they never preached, as they compete with one another in the atomized relations of the educational market place. So how can the community education movement as a whole respond to the dilemmas it confronts in an era of possessive individualism?

It would be naive to pin much hope on political change. The tide of policy is seldom turned back and, given the evidence of a widespread loss of confidence in statutory education, we need to think very carefully about what we are defending. The key elements of the 1986 Education Act and the 1988 Education Reform Act – not all of which are negative – are likely to remain in force. In some areas, LEAs with a strong local power base will struggle for their own vision of community education, but their autonomy will be seriously eroded if the present combination of centralization and expenditure capping continues. In general, it seems unlikely that LEAs as we know them will survive the combined effects of local management of schools, the internal market and the removal of further and higher education from their control. Without the strategic leadership of local government, it is difficult to see how coherent and effective policies can be defended or developed.

On the other hand, national policy does depend on local implementation. As such, it is subject to interpretation. As some of the contributors to this book demonstrate, there may be considerable room for manoeuvre here. Current government social policy has proved strong on concept but weak on detail. There is already mounting evidence of unintended outcomes and unanticipated reversals, e.g. in the Conservative government's panicked retreat from the poll tax and spirited resistance to some aspects of the National Health Service 'reforms'. Despite the claims of the new hegemony, there is apparently a strong residual commitment to old fashioned notions of equity and universalism, even 'community'.

Nor is the current restructuring of education without its problems: schools opting out of local authority control in order to opt back into comprehensive education; educational institutions struggling to collaborate rather than compete; lame ducks providing the storm troopers of the new semi-independent sector; parents becoming politicized about educational policy and finance; co-opted governors learning about the limits of the 'enterprise culture' as a model of the allocation of public goods. Indeed, Tim Brighouse (1991) argues that the subversive logic of the internal market in education and per capita funding put a premium on institutional interdependence and continuity while the demands of the national curriculum can only be managed through new forms of collaboration at the local level.

It may be that the centrally imposed imperatives of change will lead to the development of more open, accountable and democratic forms of provision. Participatory citizenship may yet prove a more practical and publicly acceptable aim for local government than privatized consumerism (Moore, 1991). The politics of practice may offer new opportunities to rework the community education movement – and to make it a more genuinely popular movement. Tony Jeffs and Mark Smith (1991), for example, claim that for the first time in their history 'community education and the community school have become oppositional'.

There is one certainty amid all the flux of change: if the advocates and beneficiaries of community education are to succeed in making a virtue out of a necessity, they must find new ways of working together in order to resolve the dilemmas of possessive individualism which now confront them.

REFERENCES

Ball, S. J. (1990) *Politics and Policy Making in Education*. London: Routledge.

Baron, S. (1989) 'Community education: from the Cam to the Rea'. In S. Walker and L. Barton (eds) *Politics and the Processes of Schooling*. Milton Keynes: Open University Press.

Brighouse, T. (1991) 'Fallacy: a national curriculum is incompatible with a community curriculum', in B. O'Hagan (ed.) (1991) *The Charnwood Papers: Fallacies in Community Education*. Ticknall, Derby: Education Now Books.

Dale, R. (1989) *The State and Education Policy*. Milton Keynes: Open University Press.

Hoggett, P. (1990) *Modernisation, Political Strategy and the Welfare State*. School for Advanced Urban Studies, University of Bristol.

Jeffs, T. and Smith, M. (1991) 'Fallacy: the school is a poor base for youth work'. In B. O'Hagan (ed.) (1991) *The Charnwood Papers: Fallacies in Community Education*. Ticknall, Derby: Education Now Books.

Jenkins, D. and Jenkins, R. (1991) *Free to Believe*. London: BBC Books.

Jonathan, R. (1990) 'State education service or prisoner's dilemma: the "hidden hand" as source of education policy'. *British Journal of Educational Studies*, **37**(2) (May).

Le Grand, J. (1990) *Quasi-Markets and Social Policy*. School for Advanced Urban Studies, University of Bristol.

MacPherson, C. B. (1962) *The Political Theory of Possessive Individualism*. London: Oxford University Press.

Moore, C. (1991) 'Reflections on the new local political economy: resignation, resistance and reform'. *Policy and Politics*, **19**(2), 73–85.

Quicke, J. (1988) 'The "New Right" and education'. *British Journal of Educational Studies*, **26**(1) (February), 5–19.

Part II

Reworking Practice

Chapter 4

Defending Community Education in Schools: An LEA Strategy

Roger Giles

In terms of local education policy development, one of the critical effects of recent legislation has been to devolve power from LEAs and to concentrate it in schools. In this chapter, Roger Giles illustrates how one LEA, Rochdale Metropolitan Borough Council – which has a long-standing commitment to school-based community education – has developed a strategy for protecting and promoting the interest and involvement of local communities in their schools. Rochdale's policy aims both to maximize the integration of 'school' and 'community' learning and to guarantee local residents their voice in the delivery and distribution of provision. The constraints imposed by local management of schools have been circumvented by means of some creative constitutional accounting. This results in a clear legal distinction between the status and remit of school governing bodies on the one hand and area-based community councils on the other, and, in effect, secures financial autonomy for the latter. Both bodies are then encouraged to work closely together to reap the very tangible rewards of collaboration. This arrangement does seem to ensure a genuine form of power sharing. It also demonstrates that LEAs which have the confidence and support of local people can retain a significant strategic role in local policy development.

INTRODUCTION

The purpose of this chapter is to describe the way one local education authority (LEA), Rochdale Metropolitan Borough Council, has attempted to defend and build upon its model of community schooling. It shows how, within the constraints of centrally imposed national legislation (the 1986 Education (No. 2) Act and the 1988 Education Reform Act), the authority has preserved the power of its school-based community councils and sought to encourage an holistic model of school-based community education.

The chapter begins with a brief summary of the aims of the authority's community education policy and considers some of the principles upon which this is based. This is followed by a more detailed description of the way community education is delivered through community schools and the role of the community council in particular. Consideration is then given to the problems posed by recent education legislation. The main part of the chapter deals with the strategic role of Rochdale LEA in developing a management strategy to ensure that its locally determined policy continues and develops and that the future of local control, through community councils, is protected.

LOCAL POLICY FRAMEWORK

The aim of community education in Rochdale is to provide a range of learning opportunities to people of all ages in a variety of community-based settings by encouraging and supporting a 'whole person' approach to education which reflects the learning needs of all members of the community. Priority is given to individuals and groups who in any way experience discrimination, are disadvantaged by the way the education system has traditionally operated, or generally have had negative experiences of education.

LEA policy is based on a set of core principles (Metropolitan Borough of Rochdale, 1989):

- People should be actively involved in the management of their own learning, making decisions not only about alternative forms and outcomes but also about curriculum development and resource allocation.
- A community development approach to education should be fostered in order to enable local people to develop together skills and knowledge as well as critical awareness about the issues which affect them and to empower them to improve the quality of life in their communities.
- Education should be organized in a way which recognizes that learning is a lifelong process and that people's educational interests and needs continue to change and develop.
- Curriculum should be rooted in the realities and resources of local community life.
- In order to make the most of educational resources within communities, systematic strategies must be developed to break down the traditional barriers between provider agencies and facilitate collaborative initiatives.

DELIVERING THE SERVICE THROUGH COMMUNITY SCHOOLS

In Rochdale most school-based community education is delivered through designated community schools. Community schools differ from other schools in the borough in that they exist to provide a focal point for the whole community and to meet the educational needs of all its members, not just those between the ages of five and sixteen. They aim to overcome the view that learning is an activity which is only engaged in by a particular age group at certain times of the day. Education can then be seen as a continuous, lifelong process and as a means of both personal and collective development.

By promoting community education in school buildings, it is hoped that the community and the school will influence each other and that a mutually supportive relationship will develop. It is intended, for example, that the curriculum of the day school and the way it is delivered will be influenced by the local community and that the school will take a lead in community development.

A crucial aim of LEA policy is to maximize local participation in programme development and resource allocation. Rochdale has a long history of community involvement in the governance of integrated community schools. Central to this approach is the community council. All community schools have a community council composed of representatives of pupils, parents, staff, governors, adult users or affiliated groups, elected members and the local community. Until the introduction of the 1986 Education (No. 2) Act all these schools also had within their instruments and articles of government a scheme of management which outlined the powers and responsibilities of both the school users and the community users. The community council, for example, was a subcommittee of the governing body with the right to representation on it. It could make decisions about the use of the building and the letting charges to be made; was responsible for the development of the community education programme; decided how to use the resources allocated to the school for community education purposes; appointed specialist community education staff; and commented on the curriculum of the day school.

Problems created by recent legislation

The 1986 Education (No. 2) Act and the 1988 Education Reform Act caused major problems for the way community education had been delivered through Rochdale's community schools. The power of the community councils, which had grown since their creation in the early 1970s, was seriously threatened; the integrated model of community schooling looked unlikely to continue and many of the service's key principles seemed impossible to implement.

Changes in the balance of power between local and centrol government, LEAs and governing bodies as well as teachers and parents pose critical dilemmas for community education policy development in Rochdale. How can the LEA ensure that community councils continue to have real power when the 1986 Act gives all the power to governing bodies and prohibits them from devolving it? If the community councils continue, how can they secure representation on school governing bodies when it is not possible to nominate such representation? How can the LEA promote a community orientated curriculum within the constraints of the National Curriculum? How can it ensure that the disadvantaged sections of the community gain access to school buildings when under local management the school has the right to let its premises to the highest bidder and generate substantial income from doing so? How can the LEA guarantee that finance allocated to schools for community education purposes is actually spent on the purposes intended?

LEA MANAGEMENT STRATEGY

The problem facing Rochdale concerned the ways in which it could implement its policy commitment to community education without contravening either the 1986 Education (No. 2) Act or the 1988 Education Reform Act. In particular, how could the principles of empowerment and integration be safeguarded? In an attempt to implement its policies and stay within the legislation, three specific measures were taken: the creation of independent community councils; the construction of a tripartite agreement; and the introduction of community education development plans.

In order to ensure that community councils could continue in their own right, they were reconstituted as independent voluntary bodies. To enable the community council to operate from a position of strength, all the extra funding that the school receives because it is a designated community school is given to the community council rather than directly to the school. In this way, a typical secondary school community council now controls more than £80 000 worth of additional funding. Provided the governing body wishes its school to be designated a community school, this places the community council in a powerful position in that the school does not receive this money unless the governing body gives the community council the right to use its school. This is the basis of the community council's power; it controls all the extra resources the LEA gives to a community school. If the school does not co-operate, the community council can withdraw its resources or even take them to another school. This, in effect, would result in the school losing its community school status.

This arrangement has been formalized into what has become known as the tripartite agreement. Both the LEA and the governing body of each school recognize the community council as the body that delivers community education in the school's catchment area. This independent community council then enters into an agreement with the LEA and the appropriate governing body, under agreed terms and conditions, concerning the use of the school. This is similar, for example, to the type of agreement entered into with the Sports Council when it puts money into schools for sports facilities. Each community council is given a set of responsibilities: to work with local people to assess the educational and social needs of its area; to develop a community education programme both within the school and throughout the community area; to support the development of new groups and initiatives; to co-ordinate community use of the school buildings and playing fields outside the normal school day; and to determine the level of charges for community use of the building. The tripartite agreement runs for four years (the duration of a governing body's term of office), at the end of which it has to be approved again by all three partners.

A crucial part of the agreement is the continuation of the block letting fee arrangement. This is where the community council pays a fixed amount per year (£5000 in the case of a community secondary school) and in exchange for this has the right to use the whole school building outside normal school hours for 25 hours per week. The community council decides who will use the premises and what charges to make, and it keeps any income. The true cost of this community use is obviously more than the amount paid by the community council if caretaking, cleaning, fuel, water and depreciation are taken into account, and the LEA meets these additional costs. Because the LEA is meeting the true cost of letting, this ensures that disadvantaged groups are not prevented from using the premises because of lack of money and that control is retained by the community council.

Various additional measures are also implemented to try to promote a more holistic model. The additional allowance that a headteacher is given because he or she is the head of a community school is now given in recognition of the additional duties undertaken in overseeing the community education programme of the school on behalf of the community council. These duties include: day-to-day accountability for the work of community education staff on the school premises; responsibility for the implementation of the school's community education development plan; monitoring and assessing the effectiveness of community education within the school; reporting to the governing body on the community education work of the school; and overseeing the management of community use of the school in accordance with the tripartite agreement. This obviously helps to ensure that an integrated and unified approach is adopted in each community school.

Each school also has community teachers who are given an extra allowance for their work with the community, the precise nature of which is decided by the community council. Teachers may apply for such community allowances on an annual basis and the interview panel consists of the chair of governors, chair of community council, community tutor and headteacher (the chair of community council having the casting vote if necessary). This encourages a compromise between school and community interests, but gives the community council the final decision if agreement cannot be reached.

Governing bodies are obviously vital within community schools, but it is no longer possible for community council representatives to be guaranteed places on them. It has been possible, however, within the process for the selection of co-opted governors to ensure that governing bodies consider nominations from community councils. In all cases to date representatives of community councils have been elected as co-opted governors.

An important element of LEA work with governors, and not just in community schools, is governor training. All governors in Rochdale are offered a six-week training course, one module of which deals with 'The school in the community'. This provides an opportunity for all governors to learn why it is important for schools to develop links with their communities, how these can be achieved, and the relevance of recent legislation to the process.

Crucial to these arrangements is the introduction of the community education development plan. All schools wishing to be designated community schools as well as existing schools wishing to retain their community status have to form a working group representative of the school staff, governors and community council. This then undertakes a community education audit of what is already happening in the school and in the community to identify gaps in provision, community needs and priorities. A development plan, based on the results of the audit and local consultation, is then produced. Once this task is complete, the development plan is approved, and amended if necessary, by both the governing body and the community council. It is then submitted to the LEA for consideration. The LEA subsequently visits the school, assesses the plan and makes a decision. Once approved, the development plan forms part of the tripartite agreement and constitutes a contract between the LEA, the governors and the community council.

Because of the importance of the development plan in the tripartite agreement, a standardized set of criteria has been produced for its assessment. For example, there must be a clear and integrated statement of aims and objectives which does not separate institutional aims from those relating to community development. The proposed management/decision-making structure should emphasize community involvement and show how all the interested parties (e.g. governors, community council members, teachers, non-teaching staff, pupils, users and elected members) will influence community school developments. It must show how the school's curriculum is informed and influenced by the school's community and its community education role. Finally, it is required to demonstrate a policy and procedure for all teaching and non-teaching staff appointments which positively acknowledges the school's community education dimension.

CONCLUSION

Recent government education legislation encourages greater public use of schools for fund-raising purposes, but mentions community schools only in passing. The only way it encourages community participation in decision making is by involving parents or co-optees on governing bodies. It does not allow community councils to continue within the school structure with any significant degree of power. It does not encourage a holistic model of the community school or a community-orientated curriculum. By emphasizing the benefits of income generation, it positively discourages schools from letting their premises to disadvantaged groups who cannot pay an economic rent. It envisages community use of schools merely as dual use of schools and does not consider the educational advantages to the pupils and the local community of more integrated approaches.

The problem facing Rochdale and other LEAs with similar community education philosophies was how to preserve school-based community education despite the constraints of centrally imposed legislation. Rochdale argued, without success, that some of the requirements of the legislation were not applicable to community schools. The only solution to the problem was to introduce new measures that would enable present practice to continue and develop.

The measures adopted were based on the belief that in any community school there are three partners that should all be involved: the LEA, the community, and the school itself. The LEA is democratically elected, and meets the cost of community education through schools; it is, therefore, entitled to ensure that its policies and priorities are reflected in practice. The community, represented by the community council, should have the right to decide for itself what form of community education it requires, identify its own needs and be involved in the delivery of any programme developed. The school (governors, teaching and non-teaching staff, parents and pupils) is also obviously a major partner in that it wishes to ensure that the education of the pupils is enhanced by the community status of the school. For this partnership to work, however, it is vital that no single partner is dominant and that they all work collaboratively for the common good.

A strategy of transforming the community councils into independent voluntary bodies, introducing the tripartite agreement and allocating additional community education funds to the school via the community council solves many problems. It allows the community councils to continue and therefore ensures that representatives of the school and its local community can continue to meet and make real decisions. It also ensures that moneys allocated to the school for community education purposes are spent as determined by representatives of the local community. The block letting fee arrangement guarantees that disadvantaged groups are not refused access to the school simply because they cannot afford to pay.

It would have been possible for alternative measures to have been taken, but those considered by Rochdale involved costs the LEA was not prepared to accept. For example, it is still possible for a community school to exist and to be totally integrated if all the power is vested in the governing body. A community council could still exist within the school, but it could only advise the governors. It could exist as a subcommittee of the governing body only if any members other than governors were not allowed to vote. The reality is that such a community council would be no more than an informal pressure group. A school which does not empower the community is not a community school.

The most important reason why the governing body of a community school should not have all the power to itself is that it cannot be representative of the school's communities, of which parents are only one element. Such an arrangement may promote efficient management by minimizing the chances of conflict, but it can only do so at the cost of effectively disempowering the community users of the school.

Rochdale chose not to go down this path. Instead, it identified clear principles, aims and priorities for the development of its community schools. The LEA's policy is based on the notion of an equal partnership between the LEA, the community and the school, and great care has been taken to ensure that this partnership remains equal. It has attempted to defend its community schools by developing a strategy based on the twin principles of empowerment and integration. Time will tell how successful this has been.

REFERENCE

Metropolitan Borough of Rochdale (1989) *Community Education: Learning in Action.*

Chapter 5

The Politics of Parental Involvement

Emma Beresford

Much has been written about the relationship between parents and teachers, home and school – by politicians (of all persuasions), academics and a vociferous, if exclusive, minority of parents themselves. Less has been heard from practising teachers, who have nevertheless had to carry the burden of all the criticism and advice from other quarters. Emma Beresford writes from long and painfully slow experience of building an educational partnership based on dialogue between the pupils, parents and teachers of an inner city comprehensive school. In this chapter she demonstrates the efficacy of genuine parental involvement – as well as the difficulty of making it work and the danger of subverting it with the simplistic and opportunistic rhetoric of 'parent power'. The account focuses on developmental work with the kind of parents, pupils, schools and communities that are least likely to benefit from the current restructuring of education on market principles. It argues that, despite the tensions between parental, political and professional agendas, the very ambivalence of imposed 'reform' presents opportunities for a new quality of partnership based upon a common understanding of the politics of education.

BUILDING AN EDUCATIONAL PARTNERSHIP

The last few years have seen major shifts in a crucial area of education. One of the key thrusts of recent legislation and an important strategy of the New Right has been to increase the power and influence of parents in education. The delicate balance between home and school has been decisively altered. This move has, not surprisingly, been interpreted by some teachers as yet another aspect of the attack on their professionalism and autonomy. In many ways it is. It is also true, however, that the need for increased parental involvement, and even power, in schools has been a cause espoused almost as much by the Left as by the Right. Why?

The fact is that home–school relations are no longer just about the obvious need for good communications: the reports, letters home and parents' evenings. They have, as Bastiani (1987) notes, 'been brought into the arena of political policy and action'.

The issues have now been stacked with hidden agendas and complex questions of responsibility, choice, control and even blame. The idea of devolving power to parents is not, it soon becomes apparent, simply in the interests of parents and their children.

Rather, as Batten (1987) suggests, it is fuelled by other motives: 'both elitists and egalitarians see the potential for the furtherance of their own educational and social objectives in the closing of the gap between home and school'.

This chapter is concerned with two major issues. First, it seems clear that this is a classic example of a matter which has been neglected (certainly in practice) by professionals and has now been highjacked for political purposes. The question is, what failures have been exposed in the process and how should teachers respond to current initiatives? Second, as a teacher directly involved in relationship between school, home and community, where does recent legislation leave me and my work? What conflicts and contradictions do I face? What opportunities can I find and what directions can I take in the future?

It is an interesting situation. It is deeply ironic that it has taken strong legislation from the Right even to bring this crucial issue to the forefront of people's busy agendas where no amount of hard work by committed individuals or rhetoric from educationalists succeeded. Parental involvement in education is at last an issue that can no longer be ignored.

It is worth briefly outlining exactly what power and influence have given to parents. What precisely is on the statute book? The 1986 Education Act significantly increased the number of parents on governing bodies, gave them a far greater say in the curriculum, and made an annual report to the parents obligatory. The Education Reform Act of 1988 followed with provision for open enrolment and opting out as well as a dramatic increase in the powers of governing bodies through local financial management. Maclure (1988) identifies the political logic of these changes: 'In future the statutory requirements for information would be reinforced by competition for pupils stimulated by open enrolment which would provide a powerful market driven incentive for a new and open approach to parents'. The legislation, therefore, seeks to work on several levels: first, through the parents on governing bodies; second, through a clear statutory requirement for schools to give information; third, through the use of market forces which, in effect, force schools to be more aware of and responsive to the wishes of parents.

It is important at this point to look at how this move towards parental involvement in schools came about. In the 1960s and 1970s there was undoubtedly something of a revolution in many classrooms. 'Progressive' and 'child-centred' education began to take root, particularly in primary schools. Many teachers became excited by and experimented with new methods: cross-curricular work; active learning; more informal relationships and more flexible approaches to reading and learning. Many of these methods were based on a recognition of the need to respect the rights of children, to enable them to have some control over their environment and to develop naturally their own creativity and desire for learning. Progressive educationalists have also often tried to give children a more connected and 'whole' experience of learning and stressed the need to enhance self-esteem, promote equality and value children's own experiences and lives.

However, while these new methods were capturing the imagination of teachers, what about parents? Often, I suspect, they were left standing at the door genuinely perplexed by the apparent chaos of the new classroom, struggling with strange words, ideas and concepts that had no echoes in their own experience of sitting in ordered rows, 'chalk and talk' and subject-based teaching. Parents were and are bemused. Lack of understanding easily leads to lack of trust.

It is here, I think, that there is a real lesson for progressive thinkers: we failed in education, as in other areas, to carry people along with our ideas. The fact is that new educational theories, with their jargon and abstract ideas, were particularly inaccessible to working-class parents and often made schools for them, even more than before, alien cultural territory.

This sense of alienation was the seedbed of the populist appeal of the Thatcherite critique and was translated into a language of educational reform which many people instinctively, if not intellectually, understood. It was epitomized by the magic words 'standards' and 'discipline'. The content of the Black Papers is well known but, interestingly, progressive methods have also been attacked by left-wing theorists in terms of their failure to meet the needs of working-class children. Green (1988) suggests: 'the instant relevance tendency . . . in earnestly seeking to meet the kids "where they're at" means you forget to take them anywhere else and leave them excluded from the culture of power'.

Whether or not standards and discipline were or are a real problem, the fact remains that teachers often failed to listen to the concerns of parents. Widlake (1986) recalls 'the patronising tone that prevailed amongst educators, the insensitivity despite their middle class advantage with which they approached their clients'.

Lack of communication and concern about standards were only factors, it must be said, within the broader context of the growing economic crisis of the 1970s, rising unemployment and a general backlash against the 'permissive' 1960s. As Dale (1989) notes:

> The . . . economic situation also began to intensify pressure for greater 'relevance' in education. It threatened the full employment basis of the [post-war] settlement and created pressure for education to contribute to the national [economic] interest rather than to the public interest.

Education became both a scapegoat for and a remedy to economic problems. New Right critics, however, capitalized on the failure of communication and fuelled concern about schools, whether justified or not. As Apple (1989) points out, they had the knack of winning adherents by capitalizing on popular sentiment. They connected with the perceived needs, fears and hopes of people who felt threatened by the range of problems associated with the crises in authority relations, in the economy and in politics. Their basic analysis is outlined by Quicke (1988):

> Central to their analysis is a view about parents' trust in the education system. Parents who rely on state education are said to no longer have confidence that their children will acquire the learning and skills which will prepare them for membership of society . . .
> This lack of trust has been brought about because LEAs and teachers, like all producers in a monopolized industry, have ceased to respond to the demands of the consumer and have abused their power. The ideology they have propagated – characterized schematically as 'curriculum reform', 'relevance', and 'child-centred learning' – has been destructive of traditional educational values with no obvious benefit to the child . . .
> The solution is to give more power to the parents by giving them the right to choose the education which they feel is most suitable for their children.

It is this analysis that has underpinned the New Right's moves towards increased parental power and choice. Four aspects of it require particular consideration: parents' attitudes to progressive education; 'parent power'; the 'failure' of teachers; and the drive towards greater parental choice.

In my own work I have, over the past four years, struggled with changes in philosophy and legislation and attempted to find a way of working which I could believe in. The practical consequences of 'parent power' and parental choice are fraught with dilemmas. How can I manage my way through what seems like a minefield, or is this even possible within the framework set by recent legislation? How do I reconcile current policy with my own practice?

First, however, a few points about the context of my work. I work in an inner-city comprehensive school in a predominantly white working-class area. My job description as a Community–School Liaison Teacher is somewhat unusual and was developed by myself and the headteacher as part of a long-term commitment to developing local people's sense of 'ownership' of the school. It was set up in the wake of the teachers' strike on the premise that good relationships between home and school are crucial to a pupil's education, that parents' lack of understanding (particularly of new methods) can profoundly affect the educational support they can give their children and that schools should have a degree of relevance to and involvement in the communities they serve.

My job is concerned primarily with developing a more community-orientated curriculum, communicating with parents and initiating a range of projects which develop community and parental involvement in the school. Since the 1988 Education Reform Act there has been an increasing emphasis on parental (rather than broader community) involvement, reflecting political changes, and – significantly – my job description has also been enlarged to include marketing, press and public relations.

Parents' attitudes to progressive education

One of the key dilemmas in my work with parents following the 1986 and 1988 legislation has been the link now forged between the attack on the teaching profession, particularly the attack on more progressive methods, and the move to give greater power to parents, especially through increased representation on school governing bodies. As Cullingford (1985) points out, 'The Government's growing interest in the role of parents comes about partly because of the realization that parents make traditional conservative demands.'

What do I do when parents strongly express a very conservative view that I believe is profoundly wrong and based on a very limited view of education, and they want me to help them to lobby the governors over it? For instance, a group of parents recently wanted to push for very traditional English teaching. As an educator, I believe that this approach would be unworkable and stultifying, resulting in pupils writing without understanding or motivation. As a Community–School Liaison Teacher, on the other hand, part of my role is to help facilitate the wishes of parents, to please the 'consumer'.

There are two ways forward, both of which arise out of the mistakes of the past already referred to. The first lies in beginning to unravel the link between parent power and traditional values. It must be said at the outset that many parents who have become involved as school governors are themselves teachers or people with progessive educational ideas. This may show how policy can backfire, but that is ducking the real issue, which is about our ability to communicate educational ideas. Most parents have only the experience of their own schooldays on which to base their judgements about current educational practice and, as O'Connell (1987) points out, these are 'for the most part authoritarian and parent-centred'. According to these criteria, teachers appear to be failing. It is interesting that even if parents' experiences of authoritarian education were very negative, they tend 'to blame themselves, not the school as an institution' (O'Connell, 1987). Macdonald (1988), on the other hand, points out that parents' ideas may well be based on a 'nostalgically remembered view of their own education' which they 'seek to have imposed on their children'.

Given this, I would argue that we need not only to explain new methods but to give parents, where possible, actual experience of them. My own attempts at this have been rewarding and stimulating. For instance, a group of parents who experienced and then discussed a series of sex education lessons were surprised about how much they learnt from methods that were far more informal, participative and enjoyable than anything they had known at school. For the teachers there was a greater understanding of parents' concerns about sex education and of how confidential information about the family should be treated. As a result, a group of teachers and parents got together to draw up a series of lessons on the family. Other projects have included parents from the school's parent and toddler group joining in discussions with pupils on discipline and safety, parents helping groups of pupils with work on small businesses, and the exhilaration of a residential specially organized for parents which combined abseiling and assault courses, assertiveness training and personal development. As one participant, a machine operator and parent governor put it: 'for the first time in my life I actually like school'.

However, the result of such initiatives is not all plain sailing; it raises problems as well as making converts. I have now been directly involving parents in secondary school education for four years and I still wonder how far it is possible to introduce new ideas and to change attitudes, battling against the pull of old memories combined with the persistent cries of the tabloids. After a brief involvement some parents have been fiercely critical of the school and its methods and their partial glimpses have given them damaging ammunition. Their attacks have often, however, contained genuine and significant concerns which need to be taken on board by the school. Others have been openly critical of individual teachers – enough to make some of them run for cover.

Overall, we have made progress and now there are certainly parents who would defend some of our less traditional teaching methods to the hilt with an understanding based solidly on their own experience. This is not to undervalue or decry the need for a constant flow of easily understood written information about educational methods, for straightforward discussion or for the snatched conversation and explanation at parents' evenings. They are equally important and obviously available to a far wider group of parents, but there is still something about personal 'hands-on' experience that breaks through prejudices and opens minds.

Winning parents over to more progressive ideas is one way of subverting the strategies of the New Right. It also, however, surely smacks of the patronizing superiority mentioned earlier: we have the right answers and have only to convince parents they are right. I would argue that unless we combine this approach with really listening to what parents are saying, we stand on very shaky ground. In my experience, there is a great deal that we can learn from the insights and perspectives of parents.

'Parent power'

The idea of 'parent power' has caused a real stir within the teaching profession, and not without reason. It has undoubtedly been adopted by the New Right in order to attack teachers, their professionalism and their misguided and supposedly 'radical' views. Within my own work, as the strategy of the New Right became apparent and parents were given increasing power through the governing body, I was faced with a dilemma. Should I even continue in a role which could be seen as facilitating this attack on the beleaguered teaching profession?

However, time and experience have led me to another perspective. What strikes me most about my involvement with working-class parents is their lack of power. Parents tend to be isolated and often full of doubts about their own role as educators. Classism hits deep, and many people experience public sector authority as intimidating and alien. These parents are faced with a highly organized and structured institution, packed full of reminders of their own anxious and often disempowering schooldays, seeped in incomprehensible language and terminology, and run by teachers who often feel threatened by their very presence.

If progressive education is about anything, it is surely about empowering those who have no power, and I would argue that in this respect working-class parents have a lot of catching up to do. Recent educational 'reform' is meant to have empowered all parents: first, in a very formal way, through representation on school governing bodies; second, some parents have been empowered in market terms through increased choice. My constituency is precisely those who are likely to have missed out in both these respects. I therefore regard part of my work as being about empowering such parents in several ways:

(a) Enabling parents to meet together to discover common ideas and concerns and to develop collective consciousness and solidarity. Through various parents' groups I have seen the relief of parents realizing they are not only the ones facing a problem. In a fourth year parents' group recently an animated account by one parent of the problems of bringing up an awkward teenager and the shame associated with attending parents' evenings was greeted with relieved laughter, echoes of similar experiences and real support. I have seen parents develop skills and confidence through organizing something together and felt them gaining strength through shared thinking. On the other hand, there has also been the in-fighting between cliques, and the sense of hopelessness about changing anything.

(b) Listening to parents and encouraging other teachers to do the same. Teachers have, after all, been trained to have all the answers, to tell rather than to listen. Entering a real dialogue with parents is likely to be a struggle for them, a lesson in lip-biting, but potentially a very enriching process. Parents' opinions on a range of subjects, from reports and records of achievement to options booklets and discipline, have given us new insights and helped to improve the effectiveness of the school. Again, my experience of this has at times been agonizing: teachers invited to come and listen to a parents' group who couldn't shut up; parents silenced by jargon and the unexpected surfacing of their own transposed sense of inadequacy and stupidity; teachers denying that their relationships with parents are anything other than perfect.

(c) Giving parents opportunities to develop both knowledge and skills. To expect any parents, except the most educated and confident, to participate in, or even begin to understand, such a highly complex and professionalized subject as modern educational practice without any training is quite unrealistic. By training I mean not only information about the education system and how it works, but also the skills and confidence to present ideas, to organize, and to achieve change and to demand accountability in a responsible and informed way. On one parents' residential course recently, at their request we had sessions on positive thinking and assertiveness and, at my suggestion, a short session on giving constructive feedback to teachers. Following this, one of the parents who had attended the residential raised an issue about homework policy at the annual parents' meeting. This had a considerable impact. Afterwards she said it was only the confidence she had gained at the residential weekend that had enabled her to speak out.

I have argued that parents – particularly working-class parents – do need to have more power and more say. But the question remains, power in what respects and to what extent? It could be maintained that working-class people should have more power, but should they have more power as parents? Should they have more say than teachers? Furthermore, should it be parents who have their say rather than the actual consumers of education themselves, the young people?

Certainly it strikes me that to increase parental involvement in decision making without addressing the question of pupil involvement is a grave mistake. Recent legislation has actually excluded young people from the governing bodies of schools at the same time as giving their parents greater representation. With all the current talk of 'citizenship' and encouragement of young people to be active and responsible members of a democratic society, this seems to be an oversight to say the least and certainly a sad reflection of the lack of respect we have for young people.

The nub of the question about parental power, however, as well as where Left and Right crucially differ, is in the extent of the 'power' to be devolved to parents. The argument that parents should have some voice in the education of their children does not seem to be in dispute; nor does the fact that good communication with and involvement of parents are likely to win their vital support and ultimately improve the performance and well-being of their children. The point that does seem to be in dispute is how much control parents should have over decision making and whether the ultimate aim is a genuine partnership or a means of policing teachers. There seem to me to be a number of arguments why parental 'control' of education should be limited.

First, there is the argument that parents must inevitably see education primarily from the perspective of their own children. Jonathan (1989) points out that education is about the actual and future interests of children in general as well as those of any particular child, and goes on to argue that since the parent cannot directly affect the social situation but only the position of her own child within it she must, as trustee, adopt a conservative social stance.

The political argument is that a 'public good' such as education is more than simply a market commodity and that consequently the whole is more than the sum of its parts. Aggregated self-interest is not enough. Those making overall decisions need to have a wider view of the good of the whole, whether it be the school or the education system itself.

Second, decisions at the end of the day must surely be made by those with most information and experience. Teaching is an increasingly complex task requiring considerable expertise. To deny and undervalue this expertise and decades of experience makes no sense – except perhaps in political terms. Third, as Cullingford (1985) points out, when we talk of parents, of course we mean a vast variety of individual human beings who do not possess a unified collective voice. Parent power within a market system inevitably means power to the strongest and most articulate and it is unlikely that the parents wielding power in many schools are in any way representative. Fourth, accountability for public services needs to be distinguished from control of them. I would argue therefore that in terms of 'parent power' what we should be talking about is not handing over power so much as increasing accountability and creating a partnership based on consultation. The crux of the matter is whether we can develop the skills and maturity, as educationalists, to listen to and incorporate the ideas and insights of parents and, indeed, other non-educationalists. Some would argue that the new governing bodies are about precisely this, but whether in practice they will fulfil this role is still open to question. Certainly, at present, we seem to have two distinct sets of parents: those on the governing bodies who have real power (potentially at least) and the rest who have no direct power at all. There appears to be little relationship between the two, apart from the annual governors' report and elections every four years.

With reference to parents as a whole – and this may well equally apply to the governing bodies in practice – it is important to be clear about what we mean by 'consultation'. Arnstein (1971) highlights in her 'ladder of citizen participation' the danger that 'consultation' may amount to little more than 'manipulation' or 'therapy' in the form of 'contrived substitutes whose real objective is to educate, correct and cure the participants'.

We also need to be very honest with parents about whether we are simply giving information or asking their opinion while retaining the power to make the final decision ourselves. It is important to be very clear about this from the outset and to give people feedback about what the final decision is, why it was made and how their opinions were taken into account. For instance, we have recently set up year parents' groups designed not only to give parents information but also to listen to their opinions about specific issues related to that year group. In one case some of the parents suggested an important amendment to a new system of reviewing that had been introduced and their role within it. I realized, somewhat belatedly, that adequate feedback was never given on the outcome of their idea.

The 'failure of teachers'

Underlying the New Right's attack on the teaching profession in general and on progressive teaching in particular is the concept of blame. This is incorporated in the thinking behind recent legislation. It is an attractively simple (or simplistic) idea: children are not emerging from school with the skills or qualifications required by society and, therefore, the adults most directly involved with young people, i.e. teachers or parents, must be to blame. The 'or' is important because it leads to a very pervasive and destructive tendency for teachers and parents to blame and criticize each other in an attempt to get themselves off the hook.

Bastiani (1987) suggests four models of the parent–teacher relationship, two of which illustrate this process of blaming. The first, the 'compensation' model, is very much the

product of the Plowden Report, which highlighted the importance of 'parental encouragement and support' to a child's educational success and raised awareness about
educational inequalities. It can also be seen as a way of blaming parents for their
children's educational failure and perpetuating the myth of parents as a 'passive, ignorant and undifferentiated body . . . needing the enlightenment of . . . knowledgeable
professionals' (Bastiani, 1987). What Bastiani describes as the 'accountability' model is
a swing in the opposite direction with teachers being blamed and parents, therefore,
being given permission to encroach on teachers' territory. In my own work I have found
this dynamic of blaming the other to be the most constantly undermining factor in any
attempt to build a partnership between parents and teachers.

To counter this it seems clear that we need to return to the original premise that only
parents or teachers are to blame – a premise which ignores the political and social
context within which parents and teachers operate. As always, the New Right banks on
our general lack of social and political awareness, and it may be that it is through
developing and deploying this that we might find a way out of the destructive cycle of
blame.

It certainly seems that some of the effect of parental involvement may not be quite
what is intended. When I asked one of the parent governors at my school whether being
a governor had in any way changed her views, her first response was that she had begun
to realize the extent to which education lacked resources. It seems that parents and
governors may in fact be beginning to realize what teachers are up against. Some, at
least, are becoming exposed to the wider issues of education policy. Interestingly, a
recent meeting of another group of parents turned into a heated discussion about local
government finance which raised questions about centralization and the 'reform' of
local government. The possibilities of a broader and more political perspective being
introduced are evident and may offer a way forward.

Another counter to the cycle of blame lies within the other two models which Bastiani
(1987) identifies in the relationship between parents and teachers: those of 'communication' and 'participation'. These cover many of the points already made about both
teachers and parents developing a genuine and mutual partnership based on listening
and understanding rather than ignorance and prejudice.

Parental choice

Both Left and the Right have supported the idea of greater parental say in education.
The key difference lies in the extent to which they think *individual* parents should be
given more power. This becomes particularly apparent when looking at the question of
parental choice. For the Right the Education Reform Act has significantly increased the
freedom of choice of the individual parent and child through policies such as open
enrolment, which make it very difficult for LEAs to assert broader considerations such
as planning policy for the area, economy or efficiency. This tension between the interests of the individual and the good of the whole reflects a dynamic often seen in the
relationship between parents and teachers, who tend to see education from different
standpoints: the former generally from the point of view of their own child, the latter
holding onto a broader view of the whole class or school. At times conflict between the
two is almost inevitable.

The New Right, however, has clearly come down on the side of concrete, specific and short-term choice for the individual, neglecting the more complex, measured and long-term view of the planner which is so vital for the efficient and equitable functioning of the whole and yet so much harder to present in populist terms. In reality 'choice' often means the choice exercised by informed, articulate middle-class parents whose 'rights' are advanced against the interests of the silent majority. Jonathan (1989) points out that some parents will inevitably have more power than others and will purchase their preferred commodity in the educational marketplace while others miss out: 'some schools will get better and others worse, with those parents who are most informed and articulate influencing and obtaining the "best buy" for their children'. In contrast, the Labour Education Bill of 1978, although it increased the weight given to parental preference, consistently gave primacy to the broader need for good education for all: 'if preference prejudiced the provision of efficient education in the area of the LEA . . . it was nullified' (David, 1987).

From the broad ideals of building community and equalizing opportunities prevalent since 1944 there is now a distinct move towards a far more limited and selective view of individual success. The shift in my own job towards 'selling' the school is part of this. One of the ironies is that I am supposed to be building a genuine partnership with parents at the same time as I am 'selling' the school. This raises the dilemma of the ethical entrepreneur. The dangers of current moves towards consumer-led education underpinned by a market philosophy are enormous. The need to market the school is fraught with contradictions.

However, as with any change, there are also positive aspects. Schools such as ours in producing promotional brochures have had to think very carefully about their strengths and weaknesses and how effectively they communicate with parents. Parental choice does undoubtedly make teachers aware of and more responsive to parents in a way they never were previously. The danger, however, is that the impetus of perceiving the parent primarily as a 'consumer' in a marketplace could lead to the involvement of parents becoming a superficial public relations exercise rather than a meaningful educational partnership.

It may be useful at this point to distinguish between the main thrusts of the 1986 and 1988 Acts. The 1986 Act was, it can be argued, primarily about increased accountability and involvement. As such, it had all-party support. It was the later 1988 Act that in a sense used the issue of parental choice to drive a 'market economy' philosophy based on competition and individualism, hence muddying the waters around what could previously have been discerned as a clear need for increased accountability and improved communication. It has also been argued that if parents felt they had greater influence in schools they would not need to choose between schools in the same way (Sallis, 1988)

I began this chapter by expressing the fear of many teachers that parents may take over their territory, using their newly gained power in an entirely self-interested way. It is a real fear and a real dilemma that are at the heart of this whole issue of parental involvement in its new politicized guise. Jonathan (1989) argues that parents naturally have this bias and that it will lead to greater injustice. Sallis (1988), on the other hand, claims that parents can both hold a broader view and, with proper information and training, also make an important contribution to the educational opportunities of all children.

Although it is hard to generalize, from my own experience and contact with many others in this field it seems that parent power may not, in practice, be the threat that many teachers feared. Parents in general do not seem to want control and are often overawed by their responsibility and all too aware of their own limitations. In reality, parent governors often feel frustrated and disempowered, excluded in practice from any real decision making and manipulated by headteachers. There remains a feeling that legislation giving parents rights to knowledge about their children's education has not gone far enough. The general picture is one of teachers struggling to get parents involved at all rather than fighting off newly 'empowered' parents.

The key threat to comprehensive education seems to be coming not so much from parents as from the New Right's other major strategy, which is the restoration of 'standards' through the centralization of control via the National Curriculum. This has, ironically, taken away considerable areas of power and choice from governing bodies as well as parents and pupils and will clearly limit how and what teachers can teach.

The New Right has undoubtedly used 'parent politics' as a means of attacking teachers and progressive educational ideas by introducing the dynamics of the marketplace into education. In particular, the 1988 Act has encouraged parents to operate as self-interested consumers in the educational marketplace. However, parental involvement *per se* is not the enemy and the basic provisions of the 1986 Act are sound: parents have for long needed to be better informed about and involved in their children's education, with schools being accountable to them for this.

It has taken legislation from the New Right to alter the balance. It is now up to us to make the most of the possibilities that have been opened up. From my own experience, I think that schools can gain enormously from increased dialogue and accountability as well as greater parental involvement and support.

There are risks and pitfalls to avoid, but the challenge is now with us as teachers. Can we at last really begin to get across to parents what we are doing in schools, and why? Can we learn to listen to the concerns of parents and consult them as partners in the education of their children? Can all parents be given the opportunities they need to take an active part in their children's education? Can we develop exciting new projects with parents and take the opportunity to pursue the unintended outcomes of a new and common political literacy about both teaching methods and educational policy? If we can, there may now be a better chance than ever of achieving a real and dynamic partnership between parents and teachers.

REFERENCES

Apple, M.W. (1989) 'Critical introduction: ideology and the state in educational policy'. In R. Dale (ed.) *The State and Education Policy*. Oxford: Oxford University Press.
Arnstein, S.R. (1971) 'A ladder of citizen participation in the USA'. *Journal of the Town Planning Institute*, **51** (4) (April).
Bastiani, J. (1987) *Parents and Teachers*. Slough: NFER-Nelson.
Batten, E. (1987) 'Attainment, environment and education'. In J. Bastiani (ed.) *Parents and Teachers*. Slough: NFER-Nelson.
Cullingford, C. (1985) *Parents, Teachers and Schools*. London: Robert Royce.
Dale, R. (1989) *The State and Education Policy*. Milton Keynes: Open University Press.
David, M. (1987) 'Reasserting parental rights to achieve economic efficiency'. In J. Bastiani (ed.) *Parents and Teachers*. Slough: NFER-Nelson.
Green, A. (1988) 'Lessons in standards'. *Marxism Today* (January).

Jonathan, R. (1989) 'Parental rights, individual liberties and social justice'. *British Journal of Educational Studies*, **37**(4) (November), 327.

Macdonald, I. (1988) A consultative document based on the Report of the Macdonald Inquiry. Manchester City Council Education Committee, September 1988.

Maclure, S. (1988) *Education Re-formed*. London: Hodder & Stoughton.

O'Connell, B. (1987) 'Families and their kids'. In J. Bastiani (ed.) *Parents and Teachers*. Slough: NFER-Nelson.

Quicke, J. (1988) 'The "New Right" and education'. *British Journal of Educational Studies*, **xxvl** (February), 5–6.

Sallis, J. (1988) *Schools, Parents and Governors*. London: Routledge.

Widlake, P. (1986) *Reducing Educational Disadvantage*. Milton Keynes: Open University Press.

Chapter 6

Equal Opportunities and Educational Values in the Assessment of Prior Learning

Beth Humphries

The ambiguity of the term 'equal opportunities' is functional. It therefore commands almost universal approbation. In reality, however, the individualistic and meritocratic rhetoric of current usage serves merely to mask and, therefore, legitimize inequalities of both condition and outcome. These are articulated in terms of class, gender, race, age and sexual orientation. In this chapter, Beth Humphries presents a systematic analysis of the New Right's distinctively politicized version of equal opportunities and a critique of its narrowly conceived economic rationale. She goes on to demonstrate, using case material drawn from her own experience of social work courses in higher education, how this can be countered at professional and institutional levels by validating the knowledge and experience which students from traditionally non-participant groups may have to offer. Positive action strategies, however, presuppose that the hidden agendas which inform and distort academic and professional thinking are exposed, problematized and reconstructed. Only in this way can the 'criteria of "excellence" make the rehearsal of personal experience a potentially intellectual exercise'.

INTRODUCTION

In recent years we have heard a great deal about equal opportunities, and current educational 'reforms' include a commitment to opening up access to higher education to those traditionally excluded from it. At the same time, recent Conservative administrations have been profoundly influenced by philosophies of the New Right, which has no commitment to egalitarian values. Indeed, the perpetuation of inequality is a central tenet of the New Right enterprise. Why then, since its philosophy is incompatible with any striving towards equality, does the present (Conservative) government tolerate the proliferation of equal opportunities policies? This chapter sets out to explore this question and to suggest ways in which the terms of the debate might be changed, and how equal opportunities rhetoric may be exploited by those concerned with social justice, in the context of developing values for assessing the prior learning of people seeking places in higher education. Such values emphasize knowledge and skills gained through life experience, particularly in domestic roles and in working-class and minority cultures.

EQUAL OPPORTUNITY: FACT OR MYTH?

At first sight the New Right philosophy which has informed policy development and the Conservative government's stance on widening access to education and training seem to be in contradiction. After all, New Right advocates believe that inequality is a prerequisite for societal development and progress, promoting property rights to the exclusion of other civil and social citizenship rights. For Hayek, enormously influential as an architect of New Right ideas, the concept of social justice was meaningless, and he argued that inequality of remuneration is a necessary condition for some members of society to invest and innovate in the interests of wealth accumulation (Hayek, 1944, 1979).

Of course, the position taken by New Right politicians and intellectuals is not new. It is grounded in and is a restatement of classical liberalism, which has come centre stage in the past decade. And although the values on which the welfare state was founded have a rhetoric of equality (enshrined, for example, in the 1944 Education Act), in fact they have been incapable of creating such equality. The stark social reality of structured inequality, thrown into relief in the Thatcher and post-Thatcher years, has been maintained with remarkable consistency over time.

'Equal opportunities' is an expression almost universally embraced but generally ill-defined and misunderstood, used to different purposes by different groups, and open to a range of interpretations. The diverse definitions account for how people from different ideological standpoints can approve the concept, and it is therefore important to consider how 'equal opportunities' is understood.

Juliet Mitchell, in *Rights and Wrongs of Women* (1976), reminds us that 'equality' always denies the inequality inherent in its own birth as a concept: 'The notions of equality, freedom or liberty do not drop from the skies; their meaning will be defined by the particular historical circumstances that give rise to them in any given epoch'. The problem is that equal opportunities can be granted in a legal sense without creating the equality of conditions for particular groups to participate. For there to be an equality of conditions, sexual, economic and racial equality have to be established. It follows that freedom in a class, gendered and racially structured society is ultimately freedom for one class to exploit another, for one gender to exploit the other and for racially dominant groups to exploit racially subordinate groups. The way this is expressed in radical conservative ideology upholds equality of opportunity in the sense that individual differences and talents may be developed, given equal opportunities, but they cannot be the basis of differences in treatment which would ensure equality of outcome. Mitchell points out that such an approach pretends that we can be equal in the public sphere when our differences are overwhelming in the private; it exhorts women to apply for good jobs, while treating babies as their private affair: 'The law enshrines the principles of freedom and equality – so long as you do not look at the particular unequal conditions of the people who are subjected to it . . .' (Mitchell, 1976).

On the one hand, the rhetoric of equal opportunities can be embraced by the New Right while those unequal conditions declared as fundamental to its project are maintained. On the other hand, anti-discriminatory legislation may be condemned as unjust in that it grants unfair privileges to minorities (Parkins, 1984). It is on such grounds that some Conservative-controlled city councils have pushed through 'reforms' whose first target has been the dismantling of racial equality and equal opportunities units.

EQUAL OPPORTUNITY OR ECONOMIC EXPEDIENCY?

There is increasing evidence of such fundamentally inegalitarian 'equal opportunity' policies and of their impact on working-class black and white women in particular. Claudia von Werlhoff (1988) links this to a new phase in capitalist development and its effects on the world economy, resulting in

> an unfree, 'femalized' form of wage labour, which means: no job permanency, the lowest wages, longest working hours, most monotonous work, no trade unions, no opportunity to obtain higher qualifications, no promotion, no rights, no social security.

Women in the UK have felt the consequences of policies which emphasize the private nuclear family in which men work while women care for children and undertake unpaid domestic work, preventing them from competing in the marketplace for jobs with men. Not that women work exclusively in the home. Indeed, since the destruction of two million full-time jobs occupied mainly by women, they are the main source of part-time employment, which suits the needs of employers for flexibility. As Veronica Beechey comments, 'the desire for flexibility takes a gendered form, and in Britain today, it is almost exclusively women's jobs which have been constructed on a part-time basis' (Beechey, 1985, p. 2). The contemporary economic reality behind equal opportunities rhetoric for women is increasingly to create a disposable unit of labour by exploiting the obligations imposed on them as wives, housewives and primary carers.

For black people in the UK, the new conservatism has meant a reformulation of old racism. Gordon and Klug (1986) document the extent to which prescriptions on 'race' have been put forward which have as their central tenets that the differences between racial and ethnic groups are inherently problematic and produce conflict, resulting in a need to keep out as many black people as possible and to assimilate forcibly those already here. Central to this thinking is the argument that it is 'only human nature' for people to want to associate 'with their own kind' and 'natural' for them to be wary of those who are 'different' (see, for example, Scruton, 1980).

A fascinating aspect of all this is the contradiction between, on the one hand, the resistance to acknowledging differences in relation to equal opportunities and, on the other, a clear attempt to construct black people as 'alien' and, therefore, to be treated differently in a negative sense. This differential treatment is apparent in a number of ways: through immigration legislation which discriminates against black people specifically (South Manchester Law Centre, 1988); through the racial imagery of crime (Gilroy, 1987); through exclusion from health and welfare services (Bryan *et al.*, 1985); through marginalization in education and training (Solomos, 1988).

The inegalitarian nature of higher education in the UK remains, and there are fears that it will increase. Williamson (1986) documents evidence to show that older people still do not get their fair share of what is on offer and that to be black, working-class or female is to be disadvantaged in the higher education system, just as it is to live north of the Trent, or to have gone to an ordinary comprehensive school. The Education Reform Act 1988 represents a revolution in education as a whole and, alongside a variety of other economic measures, its plans for higher education are a response to the worsening skills shortage in technical and vocational areas. The Act makes higher education more dependent on private money and increases the influence of industry in controlling institutions. A system of student loans has now been introduced, and also in the pipeline are plans for the variation of tuition fees in universities and polytechnics.

At the same time, there are calls for more flexibility in entry qualifications, credit accumulation and transfer and new forms of assessment, so that, given the fall in 18-year-olds, a wider range of students will be attracted, particularly women and people from black communities. In conjunction with this, the National Council for Vocational Qualifications (NCVQ) has been set up to provide national certification relating to qualifications obtained at all levels. The Training Agency's 'Enterprise in Higher Education' initiative targets people already in higher education, to direct them towards the acquisition of 'key managerial and business competencies'. But in all these cases – entry qualifications, access, credit accumulation, NCVQ accreditation and the plans of the Training Agency – people not already in work or in some form of training will be at a disadvantage. The emphasis is far more on people in employment than on an attempt to develop a creative framework for assessing prior informal learning and accreditation of such knowledge within NCVQ. Given fiscal policy's exacerbation of inequalities among those in work and the wedge driven between employed and unemployed (who are seen to have failed in the labour market), equal opportunities becomes increasingly an empty phrase.

Addressing the new social agenda

The reality is that working-class, black and women students will be deterred by the erosion and inconsistency of grant levels, the student loans system and the marginalization of the social sciences, to which a high proportion of women students have traditionally been drawn. There is little attempt to operate positive action strategies in relation to particular groups. When the Committee of Vice-Chancellors and Principals reluctantly agreed to ethnic monitoring, it did so for statistical purposes only and not for use by admissions officers. It is significant that the former Secretary of State for Education, Kenneth Baker, while pushing for increased participation rates in higher education, was unwilling to support the then National Advisory Body's proposals for a special initiative to promote equal opportunities in polytechnics and colleges. Without financial support and resources, there is no genuine attempt at access. Indeed, with an increasingly mechanistic approach to assessing prior learning, such as that suggested by NCVQ, access becomes yet another barrier to opportunity.

What then are those of us concerned about social justice to do? How can the tide of inequality be resisted, and the initiative regained to work towards greater equality in access to higher education?

Access courses

One of the ways in which entry to higher education has been facilitated is through access courses of one kind or another, though the concept is a controversial one. On the one hand, they are hailed as an important academic preparation for higher education and, on the other, they may represent yet another hurdle to be overcome. The latter refers to a danger that some people will be rerouted automatically towards access courses who could very well be admitted directly into courses in higher education given more imaginative definitions of what constitutes 'prior learning'. Later I describe an example of selection methods which aim to draw out, accredit and value informal knowledge and skills and which attempt to redefine 'qualifications' and 'experience'. In terms of class, 'race' and gender, access courses can build confidence, giving value to characteristics and experiences which many of us have been taught to regard with shame. Students confirm that, although they could have coped academically with higher education, they needed the affirmation afforded by an access course (see CNAA, 1989). The low self-esteem of some groups and the importance of developing confidence should not be underestimated.

How confusing and disempowering, then, to find a place on a course in higher education – in teaching, social work or nursing, for example – only to discover that the dominant values are male, middle-class and white. The consequences of this are that being black is regarded as a 'problem', that women's experiences are made invisible or are made marginal to men's, and that knowledge and language derived from working-class cultures do not form part of the spectrum of what constitutes 'legitimate knowledge'. Genuine efforts at opening up higher education must aim at overturning traditional notions of 'rationality', 'objectivity', 'proper' modes of expression, and so on, both in assessing prior learning and in what is regarded as 'excellence' in skills and understanding.

Admission to courses

A crucial aspect of equal opportunities is the formulation and implementation of policies on recruitment and selection. Here the picture is not entirely bleak: such policies *are* being developed. For example, Liverpool Polytechnic's policies for anti-racist education practice declare its intention of attempting to determine the ethnic origins of applicants, with a view to always granting interviews to black candidates (Liverpool Polytechnic, 1989). In some professions, particularly in the sciences, women are still under-represented and are increasingly being wooed through initiatives such as 'Women into Science and Technology'. Equal opportunities rhetoric also claims that there should be no discrimination on grounds of class, disability, age, or sexual orientation (sometimes).

However, there are a number of concerns as to how this works out in practice. The first I want to identify is a conceptual problem which has implications for practice. Feminist theorists have identified the tendency in Western patriarchal society to polarize characteristics such as male/female, subjective/objective, rational/emotional (Oakley, 1981), and thus to control behaviour and ascribe roles. In considering inequality, this tendency results in a fragmentation and masking of its reality by compartmentalizing 'oppressions' and sees them as separated from one another. Thus in social work, official documents about admission of students, for example, can now report that 'gender is not a problem' because the majority of social work students continue to be women.

What needs to be addressed, however, is the complexity of the processes of exploitation and oppression, and an understanding of the inter-relationship between the various dimensions of inequality. Such an analysis would expose the sexism of 'gender is not a problem' by identifying the absence of black women, of women with disabilities, of working-class women in social work education as well as throughout the higher education system. This polarization process leads to arguments about 'which group is most oppressed', and could lead to the conclusion that 'we have enough women on our courses'.

A first step, therefore, towards a genuine equal opportunities policy is the continued articulation of an analysis of inequality which is not reductionist in its effect, but which confronts the impact of the extent to which this society is built on and sustained by social divisions. This is especially the case in the recruitment of students, and I have been associated with recruitment drives for a social work course which acknowledged that many barriers exist for some groups in approaching institutions, and which set up an information day in a community centre used mainly by Asian women (see Shah, 1989). A black tutor and a white tutor and a number of black students were involved, publicity came through leaflets, local radio and the ethnic minority press, food was provided and a whole day was spent in informal discussions about social work and the courses available. Applications from Asian women increased as a result. This may, of course, be dismissed as a 'special case' by sceptics, but there is no reason why all courses should not publicize themselves to a wider audience through local organizations and community groups and by staff developing links with local communities. Liverpool Polytechnic's policy declares its intention of encouraging such activities across the institution. It may very well set an example others can follow (Liverpool Polytechnic, 1989).

The interest in the UK in assessing prior learning has grown, but tools for achieving such assessment are still in formative stages of development. A worrying aspect of this is to be found in official guidelines and materials issued with a view to admission and credit exemption and transfer. They are likely to adopt a rigid, technicist and mechanistic approach to the evaluation of skills and knowledge and are often couched in traditional, exclusive and unimaginative terms. For instance, Lancashire Polytechnic has published guidelines for assessment of prior learning towards admission to its Combined Studies Programme (Lancashire Polytechnic, 1988). The guidance to candidates on 'assembling your case' concerning prior learning includes 'What skills, competencies and body knowledge were acquired?' and gives as an example of 'generalizable learning outcomes' an 'ability to think and write objectively'. The evidence which students are advised to include in support of their application relates to testimonials from employers, syllabi, work experience, in-service training. None of this suggests that non-formal and informal experience and knowledge might have any relevance.

Increasingly in social work education mature candidates without formal education qualifications have been encouraged to apply for and may be accepted on courses provided they have 'some social work experience'. This usually means either employment in or voluntary work in social work agencies. It seldom means those experiences associated with being a client of the social services, or the survival skills necessary to defeat the worst effects of poverty. So, although people without formal experience in social work may be given an interview, it is only exceptionally that they are offered a place. But if women's managerial skills, for example, were to be re-evaluated, if they and other subjugated people were treated as though they belonged to society proper and their labour made central to the analysis rather than systematically excluded from it, a quite different evaluation and accreditation of 'qualifications' and 'experience' would result.

Observation of how selection takes place at interview for social work courses reveals something of the values which operate. Interviewers receive guidelines as to the kinds of qualities which are thought to be suitable in potential social workers. In most colleges and universities interviews are carried out individually by a tutor and by a social work practitioner. They also include a group interview in which candidates are observed for their skills and performance in groups. Interviewers are advised to look for an ability to be a helping person: 'in particular, can you imagine this person helping you?' It is also suggested that candidates should be 'articulate', 'good listeners', show a 'capacity to listen to others' and be neither too dominant nor too passive. The problems with these values in relation to equal opportunities will be immediately obvious. Without training in equal opportunities interviewing, images of which groups of people can be 'helpers', of who is 'articulate' and what constitutes a capacity for 'good listening' can lead to choices which exclude the very people at whom such policies are supposedly aimed. Thus some people who have been regarded as generally suitable have been rejected when a group interview revealed their strongly held views about women's issues, sexual politics, 'race' and racism, disability, ageism or whatever inequality. The justification for rejection has been not because of their particular views – that would be incompatible with 'academic freedom' – but because they were 'held too strongly', voiced too 'aggressively' and lacked 'balance'. In other words, such candidates have not been prepared to 'play the game', or have not known the rules. 'Helping', 'good listening' and 'being articulate' are defined and prescribed within unwritten class and cultural boundaries which exclude those who will not be assimilated. Sivanandan (1987) makes the point that acceptance of dominant values is a prerequisite to equal opportunities in a racist society. Philip Cohen (1988) interprets Groucho Marx's famous dictum, that he would never want to belong to a club which would have him as a member, as a direct comment on and refusal of assimilation. Is it to be only those who conform to dominant values to whom we are prepared to open the gates?

Assessment of prior learning for access to courses, which genuinely respect and allow themselves to be changed by the historical identities and the values of oppressed minorities of all kinds, has to go beyond the rhetoric to a much deeper analysis of what such assessment really means. This is a profoundly threatening prospect for institutions whose power structures depend on maintaining the status quo. However, there are signs that the NCVQ may support domestic workplace credit. Research by Linda Butler, under the auspices of the Learning from Experience Trust (*Times Higher Education Supplement*, 19.1.90), demonstrates that skills gathered in the home are relevant to study. Such skills include managerial, administrative, financial and organizational competencies.

In social work, as in some other professions, especially in teaching, a particular hot potato which threatens to sabotage equal opportunities concerns criminal convictions. Candidates are asked to declare any convictions, and a police check is carried out at the admissions stage. Some social work organizations (notably the probation service, statutory social services and most child care agencies) also carry out their own checks. This is a result of a growing awareness of the risk and extent of child sexual abuse, and such checks are necessary. But the lack of clarity and open debate about what kinds of offences should lead to rejection of candidates has allowed the definition of 'abuse' to be based on common myths and prejudices. Openly oppressive policies and attitudes towards lesbians and gay men can result in rejection, or refusal of practice placements to those who dare to be 'out' or who have convictions quite unrelated to children. Black people convicted of a single assault have found themselves the centre of panics which have attributed to them a generalized violence, with no regard for the circumstances of the incident or any understanding of police practices or the role of racism in the legislature. Reactions to such incidents are based on entirely irrational but deeply ingrained stereotypes about homosexuals corrupting and seducing children and about black people's 'constitutional disorderliness' and 'disposition to be anti-authority' (Sir Kenneth Newman, quoted in Gilroy, 1987).

Alternatively, values which promote equal opportunities for such groups would have implications for assessing prior learning very different from those on which emerging guidelines are based. An example of such values in practice is an access course to facilitate entry of people from ethnic minorities to professional courses in a social sciences faculty at Newcastle Polytechnic (Humphries, 1987). The same procedure could be adopted for entry to a range of courses at higher education level. Below is reproduced the selection methods used for entry to this course, but it should also be emphasized that these assume active recruitment through direct contact with community groups and local news media as well as a general fostering of relationships between the institution and black communities.

> In addition to supplying information about name, address, and racial origin, prospective applicants will be required to prepare a fully documented learning autobiography which will include, alongside a recording of formal education and any qualifications gained, an account of other learning showing how it was acquired, supported by whatever evidence candidates think pertinent. They will also be asked to give their reasons for applying.
>
> Written work, artefacts drawn from employment, voluntary work, home-making, references for verification will all go into a portfolio for consideration by admissions tutors. Those who are selected will be expected to continue to develop their learning portfolios throughout their access programme, where they will form the basis of assessment, and, for those who are successful, entry into professional training. Detailed guidelines as to the focus of portfolios will be supplied.
>
> In order to achieve their portfolio, applicants will attend a full day's seminar with staff . . . and will be helped to move through four stages:
>
> – identification of significant experiences which may have been occasions for learning;
> – extracting from these what it was they learned;
> – assembling evidence to demonstrate that the learning has been acquired;
> – academic assessment as to what the learning is worth in terms of level within recognized areas of study . . .

The important point about the procedure is its intention to accredit informal and non-formal learning and its recognition that candidates will need help in identifying such learning. They cannot be expected to understand that a course is attempting to apply alternative values to their selection unless efforts are made to make this clear to them. Otherwise, they will present information only about formal qualifications since they know this to be the conventional expectation.

However, such an analysis does not stop at assessment of prior learning. The changes have implications for notions of 'objectivity', for what counts as 'legitimate knowledge', for what passes as 'academic excellence' and 'standards of practice'. There is no point in valuing knowledge gained from experiences of racism in education, employment, housing or health, or of combating homophobia, or of depersonalization resulting from a label of disability, or of women's oppressions and exploitation as workers, if students are then to be told that such knowledge no longer counts once they step over the threshold into academe, where they will discover 'objective' knowledge

– much of which, incidentally, will negate and deny their experiences – upon which they will be tested and assessed.

The question of standards inevitably is raised when other than formal academic qualifications are taken into account in admitting students; but the contradiction is seldom addressed as to the shift in values which applies one set to admission and another to assessment. This can fuel resentment among traditional students against 'access' students and bring accusations of discrimination against those who have formal qualifications: 'If you're a woman or black, you're in!'. In social work training, it can also create elitism where the post-graduates are seen as the most academically able and non-graduates, particularly those on extended three-year courses (usually women with domestic commitments), are seen and treated, even publicly declared, as less able. I am not making a case for anti-intellectualism, but I am arguing that the criteria of 'excellence' need to be changed to make the rehearsal of personal experience a potentially intellectual exercise.

Such criteria should include a grasp of those theoretical perspectives which are dominant in the major academic disciplines. Yet such knowledge in itself does not bring understanding. This needs to be defined in terms of what students make of the connections between dominant theories and those commonsense and popular ideologies which shape their material existence and the lives of other social groups. To achieve this they need to be allowed to examine and explore the implications of their class position, their gender, their 'race', their sexual orientation, their ascribed level of 'able-bodiedness' and their age in an ageist society. This makes their subjective experience legitimate and highlights the hierarchical nature of British society and the ways in which unequal structures are maintained. But the analysis has to be taken even further. If an ethic of equal opportunities is to pervade their educational experience, they will need to demonstrate the practical outcomes of such a perspective in their chosen area of work. This can apply as much to the physical sciences as it can to the social sciences or the arts and humanities.

CONCLUSION

In a patriarchal society, 'community' and 'curriculum' are as polarized concepts as are 'male' and 'female'. Traditionally there has been a separation between them, with formal curricula invalidating everyday experiences because of their 'unscientific' base, and making little use of personal experience as a learning resource. Students are expected to leave what they 'know' at the front door of the university or college. Feminist theorists, among others, have set out to challenge the polarization of such thinking, to demonstrate that the 'personal is political', that theory is not separate from practice, and to work towards a synthesis which will articulate the links between them. This chapter has been an attempt to apply such insights to an aspect of higher education in the 'new age' of technological and employment-led learning. If 'community', in the sense of the knowledge and experience brought into higher education by minority and other subordinate groups, can be legitimated as a source of influence on institutional and curricular processes, then a social justice model of equal opportunities might just be in process of construction.

REFERENCES

Beechey, V. (1985) 'The shape of the workforce to come'. *Marxism Today*, **29**(8), 11–17.

Bryan, B., Dadzie, S. and Scafe, S. (1985) *The Heart of the Race: Black Women's Lives in Britain*. London: Virago.

CNAA (1989) *The Access Effect*. Council for National Academic Awards.

Cohen, P. (1988) 'The perversions of inheritance: studies in the making of multi-racist Britain'. In P. Cohen and H. S. Bains (eds) *Multi-racist Britain*. London: Macmillan.

Gilroy, P. (1987) *There Ain't No Black in the Union Jack*. London: Hutchinson.

Gordon, P. and Klug, F. (1986) *New Right, New Racism*. 37b New Cavendish Street, London W1M 8JR: Searchlight Publications.

Hayek, F. A. (1944) *The Road to Serfdom*. London: Routledge & Kegan Paul.

Hayek, F. A. (1979) *Law, Legislation and Liberty*, Vol. 3: *The Political Order of a Free People*. London: Routledge & Kegan Paul.

Humphries, B. (1987) 'Access provisions for ethnic minorities at Newcastle Polytechnic'. An unpublished discussion document.

Lancashire Polytechnic (1988) *Assessment of Prior Learning*. Preston: Lancashire Polytechnic.

Liverpool Polytechnic (1989) *A Policy for the Promotion of Anti-Racist Practice within the Polytechnic*. Liverpool: Liverpool Polytechnic.

Mitchell, J. (1976) *The Rights and Wrongs of Women*. Harmondsworth: Penguin.

Oakley, A. (1981) *Subject Women*. London: Martin Robertson.

Parkins, G. (1984) *Reversing Racism: Lessons from America*. Pamphlet published by the Social Affairs Unit, quoted in R. Lewis (1988) *Anti-racism: A Mania Exposed*. London: Quartet Books.

Scruton, R. (1980) *The Meaning of Conservatism*. Harmondsworth: Penguin.

Shah, N. (1989) 'It's up to you sisters: black women and radical social work'. In M. Langan and P. Lee (eds) *Radical Social Work Today*. London: Unwin Hyman.

Sivanandan, A. (1987) *A Different Hunger*. London: Pluto.

Solomos, J. (1988) 'Institutionalized racism: policies of marginalization in education and training'. In P. Cohen and H. S. Bains (eds) *Multi-racist Britain*. London: Macmillan.

South Manchester Law Centre (1988) *A Hard Act to Follow: The Immigration Act 1988*. South Manchester Law Centre and Viraj Mendis Defence Campaign.

Von Werlhoff, C. (1988) 'The proletarian is dead: long live the housewife!'. In M. Mies, V. Bennholdt-Thomsen and C. von Werlhoff (eds) *Women: The Last Colony*. London: Zed Books.

Williamson, B. (1986) 'Who has access?'. In J. Finch and M. Rustin (eds) *A Degree of Choice?* Harmondsworth: Penguin.

Chapter 7

Education and Unwaged Adults: Relevance, Social Control and Empowerment

Rennie Johnston

In this chapter, Rennie Johnston reflects on his own extensive involvement in state-sponsored responses to adult unemployment. His particular concern is to address the apparent contradiction between the educator's commitment to 'empowerment' and the state's interest in the educational management of unemployment. How can an intellectually rigorous and practically useful curriculum be constructed which demonstrates both the distinction and the connections between 'personal troubles' and 'public issues'? In addressing this question, Johnston draws upon the work of Paulo Freire to show how both personal development and critical analysis can be systematically fostered through the ways in which curriculum and methodology are developed, managed and controlled. Perhaps there will always be an inherent tension between participant, professional and political agendas in work of this kind. This account, however, demonstrates how these interests can be reconciled – if not entirely resolved – through a combination of 'ideological' and 'practical' action. As such, it applies to a wide variety of adult education practice with traditionally non-participant and marginalized groups.

INTRODUCTION

Mass unemployment, in prospect as well as retrospect, presents a real challenge to educators. In responding to this challenge we clearly have to identify and address the learning needs of a wide variety of unwaged adults. But this process does not take place in a vacuum. It must be seen within the wider context of a rapidly changing employment market, the vagaries and inequities of the benefit system and a dominant ideology which locates the responsibility for unemployment firmly with the individual.

My experience of educational work with unwaged adults began in 1978 with a number of suddenly redundant British Leyland workers in Coventry. Since then it has been developed largely in the Southampton area through leading two REPLAN-funded action-research projects, teaching on a number of 'second chance' courses, working part-time on an Educational Support Grant project and taking part in staff development workshops and courses with educators from many different backgrounds.

As I have developed this work, I have become increasingly concerned with what appears to be a central contradiction that runs through it: the tension between *relevance* and *social control*. On the one hand, educators like myself are anxious that our approach should be relevant and that we address the primary concerns of people who are out of work: jobs, money and security. On the other hand, we recognize that a focus on employment opportunities and coping skills can easily slip into social control, failing to challenge the underlying socio-economic structure that has created their unemployment in the first place. As we face up to this contradiction, we need also to identify positive ways of moving on from the rhetoric of empowerment towards more demonstrable ways of developing *empowerment in practice*.

In tackling these problems and in developing an approach that seeks to be relevant, critical and empowering, I have become convinced of the need for educators in this field to be clear about our own values, our working constraints, the whole social construction of unemployment and what an educational approach can hope to achieve in this context.

Educators and their socio-political aims

The Further Education Unit manual, *Adult Unemployment and the Curriculum*, has been widely recognized as offering a useful framework for understanding and developing a curriculum with unwaged adults. The manual suggests three broad socio-political aims that educators might adopt, whether tacitly or explicitly, in relating to unemployed adults (Watts and Knasel, 1985):

Social Control: reinforcing the status quo. Programmes which are concerned solely with encouraging the unemployed to enter employment, or to cope with being unemployed, might be seen as having this aim.

Social Change: seeking to change the status quo in prescribed directions. Programmes concerned solely with raising political awareness based on a particular ideological position might be understood within this aim.

Individual Autonomy: encouraging people to take as much control as possible in changing their own lives. Programmes concerned with exploring a range of options, and with respecting the autonomy of the learner, might be seen as having this aim.

How can educators avoid becoming involved in what Colin Fletcher has called 'the software of social control' (Fletcher, 1987) and take real steps towards developing individual autonomy and social change? How can we ensure that our work does not contribute only to making unemployment a little more palatable for unemployed and employed people alike? Key factors in avoiding social control have been identified as (Johnston *et al.*, 1989) helping to open up options for unwaged adults and ensuring that the curriculum is negotiable and negotiated.

However, this may not be enough. The danger is that educators help to create a cosy, student-centred, educative micro-environment that is quite separate from the 'outside world' and fails to investigate the socio-political context of unemployment and address the key questions of political power and ideology.

In the context of unemployment and its effects, the aim of social change is immediately attractive. But what is the potential for educators to promote social change? Here again there are problems. It is one thing for an educator to demonstrate solidarity with unwaged adults and to be committed to 'empowerment', but it is another to help them achieve a significant degree of power over their lives when these are circumscribed by economic pressures and anxieties, an oppressive ideology of individualism and an increasing requirement to join a government retraining scheme.

One way forward may be to differentiate between macro and micro questions. The current changes being imposed on many aspects of the education system show only too clearly where the real power and impetus lie. However, on a smaller scale, every educator can point to the personal liberation and growth that an educational approach can bring to some people. Can there be any linkage between this personal growth and wider social change?

One link may be in developing individual autonomy. This appears to be both a worthwhile goal and one that is more readily achievable! But the whole process of 'encouraging people to take as much control as possible in changing their own lives' cannot focus solely on the individual in isolation. Individual autonomy surely cannot be developed to any significant extent without taking account of the economic, social and ideological factors which inevitably restrict and limit it. Indeed, any attempt to ignore the wider context of unemployment re-emphasizes the individual over the collective and once again drifts into social control.

So how can we avoid settling for the limited and limiting role of helping to develop personal self-confidence and self-esteem while in reality leaving unchallenged the unequal and oppressive situation for those who are out of work?

A 'liberating' approach?

A potential resolution of these dilemmas may lie in the distinction that some educators have made between a 'liberal' approach to adult education and a 'liberating' one (see Fletcher, 1980; Brookfield, 1983).

The essential difference between these is that the liberal approach starts from the assumption that the individual is free, while the starting point of the liberating approach is that this is not the case, that we live in an unequal world. Any 'liberating' educational approach must first acknowledge this inequality and so be prepared to help people investigate the wider social and economic context of unemployment; that is, its economic and political causes, its economic, social and psychological effects and the range of possible responses to it at both an individual and a collective level.

Of course, there is plenty of evidence, both in educational and political circles, to show that unwaged adults are not enthused by an overtly politicizing approach. Certainly, from my experience in the West Midlands and in the south of England, one of the last things that most unwaged adults want to study is the structural reasons for unemployment. Even when such a study is undertaken, a real danger is that the objective situation can be so depressing as to be more disabling than enabling, if it is not balanced with more concrete and dynamic possibilities for personal development and growth (Usher and Johnston, 1988).

In addressing this problem, educators need to adopt a methodology which is student-centred and personal yet which takes account of the wider socio-economic context, the impact of the dominant ideology and the factors that can restrict significant empowerment. Such an approach has clear similarities to the process of 'conscientization' as described by the Brazilian adult educator, Paulo Freire:

> the process in which men, not as recipients, but as knowing subjects, achieve a deepening

awareness both of the socio-cultural reality which shapes their lives and their capacity to transform that reality.

(Freire, 1972b, p. 51)

In a UK context, I see a liberating approach to work with unwaged adults as embodying two separate but overlapping dimensions:

Contextual analysis: helping unwaged adults to develop a clear and critical awareness of the socio-economic and ideological forces that affect our lives, with particular reference to unemployment and the domestic division of labour;

Personal empowerment: helping to develop individual and collective self-confidence, personal empowerment, awareness of new options, thus identifying ways for unwaged adults to gain greater control over their own lives.

CONTEXTUAL ANALYSIS: IDEOLOGICAL ACTION

This dimension involves two central aspects. Clearly the *starting points* of unwaged individuals and groups are the most important. If they cannot be addressed immediately, any initial motivation and dynamic will be lost from the outset. A lofty 'we are not here to help you get jobs' usually gets the short shrift it deserves.

But another factor which affects individual motivation and starting points is the whole *social context of unemployment*: how it affects unwaged adults' views of themselves, their aspirations and their understanding of the labour market. This dimension is a product of the prevailing ideology projected by the government and the media which in turn influences 'commonsense' views of what is and what is not possible for unwaged adults today.

Jobs and educational needs

In relating to unwaged adults, educators concerned with being relevant often talk about responding to educational needs. The most prevalent view on this is straightforward: the primary needs of unwaged adults are for jobs and the role of education and training is to help them to get jobs. This approach underlies the work of the Training Agency, many colleges of further education and other educational institutions.

Of course, research has shown that most unwaged adults want a job as a top priority (e.g. Bryant, 1983; McGivney and Sims, 1986; Fraser and Ward, 1988) and this starting point clearly cannot be ignored or side-stepped. The problem here is the role of education. What can an educational approach realistically be expected to do? Certainly successive Training Agency schemes have been widely criticized because they are seen to train people for jobs that do not exist or develop training that is inadequate to meet the needs of either the individual or the market. What appears to be missing here is due recognition of the different circumstances and motivations of unwaged adults, a view of the whole person, and a more sophisticated and critical understanding of the dynamics and complexities of the employment market.

Economic 'facts'

A starting point in developing an alternative educative strategy is what I would call the economic 'facts' approach. It begins by acknowledging and addressing the identified need of unwaged adults for a job and all the other things that go with it: money, personal value, self-esteem and so on. However, any joint educational investigation of that goal has to examine the nature of the employment market, as this has a clear bearing on the skills, knowledge and attitudes that a person has to possess or develop in order to become employed. The economic 'facts' that emerge from such a joint investigation are that:

-   there are not enough jobs to go round – even in areas of high employment, the number of people unemployed usually exceeds the number of vacancies;
-   there is a clear mismatch between the skills that the 'market' requires and the skills available among the unwaged; there are many practical barriers that keep people out of the workforce, such as the need to care for children or elderly relatives, or transport problems.

In this way, the context of unemployment is addressed while, at the same time, relating to identified needs. This does not necessarily deflect any unwaged adults from pursuing the goal of employment, but it does address wider socio-economic factors and helps individuals to analyse the labour market, to understand better the structural (and political) reasons for unemployment and hence move away from ideas of bearing the prime responsibility for their own unemployment. In this way, unwaged adults can begin to become in Freirian terms 'knowing subjects' (Freire, 1972b).

Self-employment within an enterprise culture

Of course, it can be argued that the labour market is changing and, as a direct result of this, our new 'enterprise culture' offers a wide range of employment opportunities for unwaged adults. How should educators respond to the upsurge of interest in this approach?

In this context it may be useful to take note of Freire's analysis:

> There is no such thing as a neutral educational process. Education either functions as an instrument which is used to facilitate the integration of the younger generation into the logic of the present system and bring about conformity to it, or it becomes the 'practice of freedom', the means by which men and women deal critically and creatively with reality and discover how to participate in the transformation of their world.
>
> (Freire, 1972a)

With this in mind, educators need to treat the values and language of an 'enterprise culture' as problematic. So in addressing self-employment, educators should recognize that it clearly holds out a vision of independence, freedom and autonomy. As such it may be genuinely attractive to those with skills, flair and ambition as well as those who are disadvantaged in the labour market, e.g. women, the black community, the housebound. It is seen by many part-time or frustrated employees as a liberating first step away from the unsatisfactory jobs they are trapped in.

However, educators also have the duty to point out that in order to be 'successful' you need to have marketable skills, good contacts, a capital base, and lots of time, personal drive, determination and hard work. The price of independence and freedom is often total commitment, increased debt and anxiety and further insecurity. Another significant 'economic fact' is that at least 50 per cent of new small businesses fail within four years. Such a problematization of the values and language of an 'enterprise culture' may persuade some people at least to look before they leap into a decision that could be wrong for them, and ultimately wrong for the economy.

Adult education and unwaged carers: education for 'work'?

So far, much has been made of an educational response to the needs of many unwaged adults for paid employment. However, not all unwaged adults are in a position to have this as an immediate goal. They may be restricted by domestic responsibilities, such as looking after a child, parent or disabled relative. How can an educational approach be made relevant to their needs and circumstances without condemning them to a diet of 'coping skills' and traditional non-vocational provision?

Perhaps a way forward is for educators to help re-examine the whole concept of 'work' and to move away from unhelpful distinctions between paid employment and 'non-economic' activities. Many have no time to consider paid employment in the short term but still have legitimate ambitions for the future. An adult education approach to unwaged adults can acknowledge clearly that carers are indeed 'at work'. This can help us avoid the traditional but false dichotomy between vocational and non-vocational courses and talk simply about 'education for work', where work is seen as explicitly covering a whole spectrum of caring, housework, self-employment, as well as more conventional employment. In this way, the work that many unwaged adults already do will be properly validated, and clearer progression outlined to paid work and other areas of personal development and growth.

PERSONAL EMPOWERMENT: PRACTICAL ACTION

A problem-posing, economic 'facts' approach still needs to be balanced by more personal and developmental work if there are to be real opportunities for unwaged adults to gain greater individual autonomy and start to try to take more control over their lives. For educators, key factors in developing such a personal and developmental approach are appropriate methods of contact, forms of negotiation, learning environments, attitudes to knowledge, access to resources and individual and collective progression routes.

Contacting unwaged adults

An important starting point for the educator is making meaningful contact with unwaged adults in the first place. Two main methods of contact are normally used. The first, an outreach approach, involves going out to identify and engage unwaged adults on their own 'territory', at unemployment centres, mother and toddler groups, in the local community. The second, a marketing approach, focuses more on 'selling' the idea and relevance of education to unwaged adults through a variety of publicity media or institutional contacts, perhaps through the local Job Centre. In developing the most appropriate method for contacting unwaged adults, educators need to be aware of the implications of using different methods.

The dangers of a marketing approach are that it can become essentially consumerist or, in economic terminology, 'supply-led'. Current economic pressures and existing budgetary constraints and targets often make it very difficult to embark on any long-term marketing strategy that goes beyond developing a token dialogue with non-traditional student groups. The result can often be that the unwaged adult is allocated a passive role in making a purely reactive choice from a limited 'menu' of educational possibilities.

In contrast, an outreach approach may be less concerned with finding a market for its potential educational provision (supply/institution-led) than making education responsive to the prevailing concerns and interests of those in the local community (demand-led). It tries to move away from ideas of educational consumerism and to view the educational process as much more of a dialogue. In fact, it aims to go beyond immediately articulated wants to discover latent needs over a longer period of time. This clearly involves a process of negotiation.

Negotiation

The idea of negotiation recognizes that each partner to the negotiation process has something to contribute to the eventual outcome. This recognition is clearly both 'politically' and practically important if educators are to move away from any idea of a 'deficit' model of unemployment and acknowledge that unwaged adults have valid knowledge, experience and ideas that must be taken into account in developing an educational approach with them (Usher and Johnston, 1988).

Of course, negotiation is not simply a one-off interchange. It is a complex process which seeks to explore the needs and wants of unwaged adults and how an educational approach can (or cannot) respond to these. It involves the educator establishing dialogue, credibility and trust, and unwaged adults becoming confident enough to take an active part in the learning process. It needs to be developed over time and in a supportive environment.

The learning environment

An important factor in promoting this personal development and progression is the nature of the learning environment. The whole issue of access has moved up the educational agenda in recent years. However, there are two sides to access: one is identifying and devising different routes that (unwaged) adults can take to gain access to traditional knowledge and progress up the educational ladder; the other is tackling the root problems that limit access. Not surprisingly, educational institutions are usually better at 'routes' than 'roots'.

There may be an analogy here between educational and economic strategy. The dangers of concentrating on 'access' courses in an educational context are similar to the dangers of concentrating on stimulating demand and economic growth in the economy. Those with existing educational (and economic) capital may make use of such access courses, but unwaged and other oppressed groups may not be able to take advantage of the new opportunities. In both cases, what is neglected is the vital infrastructure necessary to take account of the starting points of the most marginalized members of society.

Table 7.1 gives an indication of some of the barriers that exist for unwaged (and other) adults. Only when the educational infrastructure is developed to take account of these barriers will real access be possible for many unwaged (and other) adults.

Table 7.1. *Barriers affecting the unwaged*

Barriers to access	Examples of groups affected
Money	Poor unwaged
Value dominance (race, gender, social class)	Black community, women, working class
Child care	Single parents, women
Physical disability	Physically disabled, deaf, blind
Bureaucracy	People without confidence, with limited time
Timing	Shift workers, part-time workers
Information	People without access to existing information channels
Language (in publicity)	Those put off by formal English
Language (in learning)	Non-English-speakers
Previous education	People with negative school experience, without qualifications
Location	People with personal commitments, without private transport
Ownership of resources	People too dependent on institutions for resources
Previous experience	People depressed by their own situation; for example, unemployed
Lack of confidence	People who think or have been told they could not cope with a particular subject
Inappropriate structure of courses	People unable to progress from ABE to GCSE or other provision
Irrelevant content	People wanting to or needing to relate learning to their own life

Source: Cowperthwaite *et al.* (1989, p. 3).

Tackling these barriers involves fundamental changes of attitude on the part of educators and institutions and a real commitment to equal opportunities. It also involves challenging many traditional curricular assumptions.

Knowledge, education and empowerment

A key question to be addressed in trying to develop any kind of 'conscientization' approach is the relationship between knowledge and education. Freire is very clear that education for liberation must move away from what he calls the 'banking concept' of education and resolve the 'teacher–student' contradiction:

> In the banking concept of education, knowledge is a gift bestowed by those who consider themselves knowledgeable upon those whom they consider to know nothing. Projecting an absolute ignorance onto others, a characteristic of the ideology of oppression, negates education and knowledge as processes of inquiry. The teacher presents himself to his

students as their necessary opposite; by considering their ignorance absolute, he justifies his own existence.

(Freire, 1972a)

How can we develop in practice a very different educational process, given the constraints of educational institutions and the background and traditional expectations of many unwaged adults?

An empowering educational approach involves a critical view of conventional knowledge, but it also needs to develop methods that are genuinely student-centred. Certainly, lessons can be learned here from many significant developments in women's education with its emphasis on an experience-based curriculum and its refusal to separate the emotional and intellectual aspects of learning. Similarly, Open Learning in its broadest sense (i.e. not just access to conventional learning packages) offers models of learning that are potentially student centred and empowering.

Another point of reference may be the idea of a learning exchange. This explicitly recognizes the knowledge and skills that people bring with them and immediately refocuses the educational dialogue away from institutional knowledge to personal knowledge. Instead of starting from what (unwaged) adults want or need to learn, they can be asked what they have to offer in terms of skills, experience, knowledge and ideas (see Johnston, 1984). The dialogue that this often prompts is immediately a more equal one and can help to start the process of seeing education in a different, more interactive and dynamic light.

A learning base for unwaged adults

A vital factor in translating this interaction into practice is the availability and 'ownership' of resources. While a learning exchange approach can begin to raise confidence and educational consciousness, only resources that 'belong' to (unwaged) adults can make a learning exchange work and help overcome the natural suspicions that many unwaged adults have of educators. Furthermore, open-access workshop and self-study resources can help people to start 'doing' education and so see it not just as an intellectual activity but as essentially practical, personal and immediately accessible. From this starting point, with good information sources and supportive educational advice and guidance, people can begin to identify different ways of developing their learning and lives, whether individually or collectively (see Johnston, 1987). In this kind of learning situation a supportive educator is clearly acting very much as a 'teacher/student' alongside 'student/teachers' (Freire, 1972a).

A learning centre that helps to raise confidence and develop skills among unwaged adults, relate individual needs and interests to wider socio-economic circumstances and open up options for different individuals can assist people to 'progress' in the education system or in other chosen directions, such as jobs, voluntary work or community action. However, there is still the danger that this kind of programme helps unwaged adults only to change their lives on a strictly individual basis (if at all) and does not alter their collective position. Certainly in the present political climate it is often difficult to identify any way forward that would help to develop collective empowerment without raising expectations that may only be dashed against the power of wider economic forces. One possible first step in the right direction may be in the organization and management of the learning facilities available.

Much of the rhetoric of participation and empowerment can be made a reality if unwaged adults have real power over resources and the base in which they learn. There are good examples of this from work initiated through REPLAN projects and continued with LEA and other backing. For example, the Respond Base in Southampton (Johnston, 1987) and the BUG and BRAG groups in Wolverhampton (Groombridge, 1987) have shown how the solidarity that is often typical of unemployment centres can be combined with an educational approach that encourages unwaged adults to share and develop skills, to 'own' and develop learning resources and to make decisions about the organization and running of their working-bases. In all these examples, decisions about the day-to-day running of the base, the use of resources and overall policy are made by unwaged adults at regular meetings.

This function of management and control not only gives unwaged adults a real experience of empowerment within the learning centre but it can also form the beginnings of a wider exploration of power in dealing with funding organizations, local educational hierarchies and local government structures. Thus unemployed groups can have a voice within the local community, can build up supportive networks with other groups and agencies, and individuals and groups can gradually develop new negotiating, lobbying and management skills, with support from educators if required.

Different educational contexts

The approach outlined above may be best suited to a community-based learning centre specifically intended for unwaged adults. However, a variety of educational institutions can benefit from such a way of working, and develop close links with unemployment centres and groups so that, where appropriate, unwaged adults can have access to a wider range of educational options.

Furthermore, other educational institutions can perhaps borrow some key working principles. For example, if colleges are really serious about relating more positively to unwaged and other adults among their 'new client groups', they need to develop their outreach contacts and credibility as well as their educational infrastructure (such as the provision of a crèche, or disabled access). They could also attempt to develop a workshop-style learning exchange approach and more comprehensive and personal educational advice and guidance. Even 'ownership' of resources and more directly democratic structures could be encouraged. A more imaginative learning base could broaden the whole concept of 'open learning' and in so doing provide a necessary link with outside values and attitudes and a stimulus for changing the traditional institutional culture of a college.

CONCLUSION

In order to be 'liberating', educational work with unwaged adults should embody both an ideological dimension and a more practical and personal dimension. In this way, educators can combine a critical analysis of society and the reasons for unemployment with a more student-centred methodology which addresses the starting points and concerns of unwaged adults and takes account of the limits and the constraints of specific working contexts. It is possible for educators to help unwaged adults become more critical of the dominant ideology and at the same time achieve greater individual and collective autonomy.

The potential contradictions and tensions inherent in educational work with unwaged adults are considerable. In order to resolve them, educators who commit themselves to a 'liberating approach' need to become involved in a continual process of action and reflection with unwaged adults.

As educators we cannot expect to solve all the problems of unemployment or fundamentally alter the overall oppression of the unwaged. But we can avoid colluding in social control; we can make education both relevant and empowering. Indeed, we may even help to establish a base for change:

> The materialist doctrine that men are products of circumstance and up-bringing, and that, therefore, changed men are products of other circumstances and changed upbringing, forgets that it is men that change circumstances and that the educator himself needs educating. (Marx, quoted in Freire, 1972a)

REFERENCES

Brookfield, S. (1983) *Adult Learners, Adult Education and the Community*. Milton Keynes: Open University Press.
Bryant, I. (1983) *The Educational Needs of Long Term Unemployed Adults*. Glasgow: University of Glasgow.
Cowperthwaite, P., Johnston, R. and Ryves, M. (eds) (1989) *Access in Action: Breaking Down the Barriers*. Leicester: NIACE Replan.
Fletcher, C. (1980) 'The theory of community education and its relation to adult education'. In Thompson, J. (ed.) *Adult Education for a Change*. London: Hutchinson, pp. 65–82.
Fletcher, C. (1987) 'The meanings of "community" in community education'. In G. Allen, J. Bastiani, I. Martin and K. Richards (eds) *Community Education: An Agenda for Educational Reform*. Milton Keynes: Open University Press, pp. 33–49.
Fraser, L. and Ward, K. (1988) *Education from Everyday Living*. Leicester: NIACE Replan.
Freire, P. (1972a) *Pedagogy of the Oppressed*. Harmondsworth: Penguin.
Freire, P. (1972b) *Cultural Action for Freedom*. Harmondsworth: Penguin.
Groombridge, J. (ed.) (1987) *Learning for a Change*. Leicester: NIACE Replan.
Johnston, R. (1984) 'A learning exchange as part of community education'. In *Education for Adults*. Open University Unit 355. Milton Keynes: Open University Press.
Johnston, R. (1987) *Exploring the Educational Needs of Unwaged Adults*. Leicester: NIACE Replan.
Johnston, R., MacWilliam, I. and Jacobs, M. (1989) *Negotiating the Curriculum with Unwaged Adults*. London: Further Education Unit.
McGivney, V. and Sims, D. (1986) *Adult Education and the Challenge of Unemployment*. Milton Keynes: Open University Press.
Usher, R. and Johnston, R. (1988) 'Exploring problems of self-directed learning within practice and discourse', *Studies in Continuing Education*, vol. 1. Kensington, NSW: University of New South Wales.
Watts, A.G. and Knasel, E.G. (1985) *Adult Unemployment and the Curriculum: Manual for Practitioners*. London: Further Education Unit.

Chapter 8

'Straightening the Bend': From Psychiatric Hospital to Care in the Community

Liz Foster

Large psychiatric hospitals may seem unlikely places for a genuinely developmental and person-centred adult education practice to evolve. Nevertheless, this account shows how the internal community of the 'total institution' can generate a distinctively liberating form of curriculum and pedagogy. These are difficult to replicate as patients are moved out of the asylum of the hospital to live in an external community which is at best ignorant and uncaring, at worst prejudiced and hostile. Liz Foster recognizes the ambivalence of 'community care' policies. She argues that real care in the community is predicated upon not only the education of lay members of the wider community about mental illness but also the deschooling of competing professional and institutional ideologies of caring. 'Straightening the bend' between the mentally ill and the wider community also means addressing collective interests and needs which are all too easily submerged within the pervasive individualism of conventional thinking about education and caring.

THE EDUCATIONAL IMPLICATIONS OF THE MOVE FROM THE 'TOTAL INSTITUTION' TO 'COMMUNITY CARE'

> Patients were said to go 'round the bend' because many mental hospitals were built so that they were hidden from the community by a bend in the road.
>
> (Geoffrey Baruch)

This chapter is written from two different perspectives. It is based on my experience both as a Health Service employee working within a large psychiatric hospital, and as a lecturer in a college of further education, where I currently have responsibility for developing educational provision for adults with mental illness and/or behavioural problems. Like so many of the patients, I have made the move from the security of the institution to the outside world with its inevitable risks and uncertainties.

> I came for shelter at a bad time for me and shelter I have had. (Hilda)

The psychiatric hospital comes under Goffman's umbrella definition of a 'total institution': 'a place of residence and work where a large number of like-situated individuals, cut off from the wider society for an appreciable period of time, together, lead an enclosed, formally administered round of life' (Goffman, 1968). The roles of those who live and work within the 'total institution' are clearly defined. Within the psychiatric hospital, trained staff are there to ameliorate the patients' illnesses; the patients are there to be treated.

My role as an educationalist within a large psychiatric hospital – while being outside the medical model of illness and treatment and thus outside the professional hierarchies of the psychiatrists, clinical psychologists, occupational therapists, nurses and social workers – was essentially one of *preparation*. The patients, after years of institutionalization which had robbed them of the ability to make choices and decisions at even the most basic level, were being prepared for life in the wider community in line with the government's policy of closure of large psychiatric institutions and movement to 'community care'.

The concept of 'community care' has been embraced enthusiastically by all political parties since the 1959 Mental Health Act first announced plans for the closure of large psychiatric hospitals. The apparently warm and friendly connotations of 'community care' may mask a colder and starker reality: the concept appeals to those who have a vision of an ideal society in which the able-bodied care for the infirm and elderly; it appeals to the desire to promote independence and self-help; it has attraction as a cost-cutting exercise. *The Hospital Plan for England and Wales* (Ministry of Health, 1962) and *Health and Welfare: The Development of Community Care* (Ministry of Health, 1963) firmly established the principle of community care for the elderly, mentally ill and mentally handicapped. The concern was with care *in* the community not *by* the community, with the implication that any care which took place outside an institutional setting was intrinsically better than that which took place within it.

By 1981, however, with ever-increasing constraints on public spending and the ideological critique of 'welfare dependency', the emphasis shifted from care *in* the community to care *by* the community. *Care in Action* (DHSS, 1981), reflects the new stress on informal care. This was reiterated by Kenneth Clarke, then Secretary of State for Health, in his response to the Griffiths Report, *Community Care: Agenda for Action* (Griffiths, 1988) on 12 July 1989:

> The great bulk of community care will continue to be provided by family, friends and neighbours. The majority of carers take on these responsibilities willingly and I admire the dedicated and self-sacrificing way in which so many members of the public take on serious obligations to help care for elderly or disabled relatives and friends.

In effect, care by the family usually means unpaid care by women within the home. There are many who take on this continuous burden of responsibility even when they are old and frail themselves, but the increasing fragmentation of the nuclear family through divorce, remarriage and single-parent families prompts the question (Walker, 1983): 'Who will care for the step-grandfathers and step-grandmothers of the next century?'

While it must be borne in mind that ninety per cent of caring always has taken place in the community, my concern focuses principally on the small percentage of people who, as a result of mental illness, have been institutionalized for significant periods of their lives. Many no longer have families to care for them in the home. What they need is care in the community which can offer them all the support and asylum which was provided by the large mental institutions – and more besides.

Community care has developed in a piecemeal fashion, depending on the priorities of individual health and local authorities. It was not until 1985 that regional health authorities were asked to submit plans to the Minister of Health regarding the closure of these hospitals and proposed alternatives such as community mental health centres. The current political orthodoxy, in line with the Griffiths Report and reiterated in the White Paper *Caring for People* (Ministry of Health, 1989), is that NHS and local authority community care provision should be minimal. Instead, local authorities should have the responsibility for establishing and monitoring contracts with whichever agencies they consider able to provide the most appropriate care.

By 1991, every district health authority was required to have co-ordinated care programmes for people with mental illness who were being discharged from hospitals. Yet those local authorities which had historically accorded mental illness low priority had started from a low base of suitable resources with little time to develop an adequate service. Thus the level of community care remains variable throughout the UK, with the services provided by local authorities and voluntary bodies forming an important part of the total picture.

In reviewing these trends, it is easy to forget the human element, the people who have for many years been institutionalized and forgotten. The current situation for many of them is exemplified by an anecdote about the murals in an elderly persons' home which formed part of a slide show depicting community arts work. The first slide showed an unattractive mural depicting an industrial landscape. The second showed the same wall covered by a new mural of a seascape with billowing clouds and rolling sea. Beneath the new mural, however, was a row of chairs arranged so that the elderly people occupying them were facing away from it. Undoubtedly, the second mural was an improvement – but the question remains: did the residents want a mural at all?

A similar question arises in connection with the movement of long-stay patients from institution to community. It is often hard for them to feel that the preparation for and movement to the wider community is, in fact, what they want. The closure of the large psychiatric hospitals is depriving them of the very community in which they have spent a large part of their adult lives. This internal community has provided them with shops, cafes, entertainment, work and pleasant grounds to walk in. Less obviously, it has provided a social network, formed through determination and resilience, which embraces friendships, sexual relationships and business ventures. It has also offered asylum at a time when external pressures have become too great to bear.

Far from concluding that institutionalized living should therefore continue, cut off from the rest of society, I would argue that good care in the community must take account of these positive aspects of life within the institution. It is far from easy for patients to become integrated into the wider external community in which they have lost the family ties, social roles and relationships they once possessed.

The education of long-stay patients within the institution initially has to be, to a large extent, directive. People who cannot make informed choices about their future because they no longer have any realistic points of comparison between life within and outside the hospital cannot, by the same token, easily make choices about their educational needs. For example, it would be virtually impossible for them to make a realistic appraisal of the level of literacy skills which they would need in order to cope to their satisfaction with practical and emotional aspects of life in the outside community. Thus, initially, the possibility of the student-led curriculum is impractical. Yet at the same time I do feel that it is possible to work towards greater autonomy and empowerment.

Just as Hargreaves (1982) suggests that 'we might take as our principal aim for secondary education the promotion of dignity' so, arguably, the aim of education in rehabilitation should be to restore a sense of self-worth to people whose dignity may have been damaged by the relatively impersonal and inflexible routine of hospital life.

This involves developing curriculum and pedagogy in ways which reflect a particular understanding of the educative community:

> The definition of 'community' is crucial because it implies a critical choice between an essentially hierarchical, socially regressive and static model of social relations and one that is progressive, emancipatory and dynamic.
>
> (Martin, 1987)

It means refusing to see

> the illiterate . . . as a sort of 'sick man' for whom literacy would be the 'medicine' to cure him, enabling him to 'return' to the 'healthy' structure from which he has been separated.
>
> (Freire, 1972)

This kind of educational commitment runs directly counter to the institutional culture of the psychiatric hospital. Here education tends to be seen as a process of schooling that is inappropriate to the needs of institutionalized, often elderly, patients because it is primarily concerned with transmitting a fixed body of knowledge that

> has come to belong to particular professions which require a specified length of training to master and possess it, before an individual can be seen as making a legitimate contribution within the service system. Positions in the hierarchy and knowledge are closely linked and given authority and legitimacy by the ideology of an 'expert-led' service.
>
> (King's Fund, 1988)

It was this view which our literacy project within the psychiatric hospital aimed to counter by giving validity to the lived experience of people who had lost self-confidence and self-respect. It involved establishing initial progress in reading and writing by using the students' own words, enabling them to 'read the world' (Freire, 1987), *their* world, and through reading it and writing about it to come to know it better. It also involved establishing writers' workshops, which provided another channel for new voices to be heard, the voices of people whose stigmatizing illness and institutionalization had rendered them powerless. Gradually, people began to see themselves no longer as patients but as students and writers, learning and sharing together.

We endeavoured to redress the balance with regard to the usual unequal power relations between patients and members of staff. The groups slowly became more student-led and topics were increasingly chosen by group members. We took our first steps together into community publishing and radio broadcasting – stemming from one group's decision that collectively they could write one-act plays at least as good as the ones we had been reading together.

We introduced a wealth of English literature to which the students had a right of access that had long been denied. Wartime reminiscences were accompanied by reading the First World War poets; discussion of the supernatural involved extracts from *Macbeth*; sharing experiences of hospital life included looking at Elizabeth Jennings's poetry; a whole project on the Poet Laureates was requested.

A play-reading group was set up in response to a request for an evening activity which would appeal to those people who did not like playing bingo (Foster, 1988). The members of the group, drawn together by a common interest, became firm friends, and we included trips to the cinema and theatre in our weekly meetings. The usual ward outings tended to embrace films such as *Bambi* and annual theatre trips to the pantomime. Our group's choice included Brecht's *Mother Courage and Her Children* and Alan Bleasdale's *It's a Mad House*.

The literacy project room also came to be used as a drop-in centre by patients who grew to appreciate the lack of formality and knew that there would be a variety of reading, writing and drawing materials available for use, with or without the help of a tutor. Moreover, there were always plentiful supplies of tea and biscuits. It was here that 70-year-old Lewis, admitted to hospital thirty-two years earlier and remaining mute for much of this time, learned to make a pot of tea, read the daily newspaper and comment on the football results which he had read. On his ward, however, tea (with milk and sugar already added) would be served by the staff at set times and one newspaper would be provided for the whole ward. We were, of course, fortunate that we could work with such small groups of people and consequently could offer so much more individual attention to our students.

The introduction of the computer and word processor facilitated the production of writing which had a professional appearance, thus giving further validity to the patients' work. Moreover, it gave them back a right that had long been denied them, the right to become familiar with new technology and to gain 'hands-on' experience of equipment which initially appeared to be complex, confusing and threatening.

Education of the community

> Everyone knows what it's like to crack up. (Leonard Cohen)

In considering the needs of the mentally ill as they move from large psychiatric hospitals into the community, it is easy to forget that the community may, in fact, be less than welcoming. By and large, public interest in psychiatric institutions since the compulsory erection of county asylums in the late nineteenth century has remained slight. From the time of the Lunacy Acts of 1890 and 1891, which introduced certification of unsoundness of mind, until the 1930 Mental Treatment Act, which allowed people to be admitted without a compulsory order, there was no legislation protecting the rights of psychiatric patients. Indeed, it was not until the 1959 Mental Health Act that changes in the status of patients and an open-door policy were introduced. Thus psychiatric institutions became, in effect, places where the troublesome, the misfits could be put away and society relieved of the inconvenience of having to care for them. It is not surprising, then, that myths, prejudices and misconceptions about the nature of mental health problems have become rife over the years. Little was known of what went on behind the high walls and locked doors. Still today the media show a much lower level of awareness and respect towards people with mental illness than is now afforded to other minority groups. Images of mental illness depicted in the popular press reinforce people's fears and stereotypical images.

Moreover, there continues to be considerable confusion about the difference between mental handicap and mental illness, with the two terms often being used indiscriminately and interchangeably. In fact, mental handicap is a state of arrested or incomplete development of the mind which affects the intellect, whereas mental illness is a disturbance of mental processes which disrupts a person's life. Anyone can become mentally ill – it is no respecter of class, gender, race or status. It may well be that the very reason we are reluctant to talk about mental illness is

> an almost unconscious recognition that no harsh dividing line separates them from us, that we share to some degree their anxieties and traumas and that we are more at risk than we care to contemplate.
>
> (Webb, 1975)

Consequently, a vital step in any community care policy must be to educate the community about mental health and mental illness in order to break down the barriers of fear and misunderstanding, remove the stigma which is still attached to mental illness, and enable the integration of the mentally ill to occur in a meaningful and positive way.

At the college where I am now based a 'Know Your Neighbour' course has been run for several years to educate local people about the mentally handicapped who have been resettled into the community. We have now extended the course to cover mental illness, thus affording ourselves an opportunity to highlight the difference between the two conditions, and we are offering it to college staff as well as members of the wider community. Our aim is to provide information about the effects of institutionalization, current community care policy and the range of support services available, in addition to allaying widely held fears and misunderstandings. We are assisted by health authority and social services staff both through their contributions to the course and through their willingness to receive interested visitors in their places of work.

Education in the community

> 'Somebody told me I was moving to Duncan Street . . . I was glad when I got there . . . I've got me own bedroom and bathroom . . . This is the best place I'm in.'
>
> (Joan, after 35 years in hospital)

The movement away from the institution to the community brings with it a blurring of roles and aims. The professionals lose the power bases which they had within the institution and their clearly defined roles. Moreover, aims need to be rethought, preparation being replaced by integration. This involves an important shift of emphasis since there is a qualitative difference between the functional, task-orientated, hospital-based approach to resettlement and a process-orientated, community-based approach which involves facilitating access to activities and services which are also available to other members of the community. These changes cannot be accomplished successfully without interdisciplinary support and understanding. Staff development needs to take place in a multidisciplinary setting (Roberts, 1987), thus preventing each type of professional from formulating the problems of the mentally ill 'merely in terms of his or her own particular expertise' (Richmond Fellowship, 1983). Roberts (1987) describes how six members of staff from four Liverpool colleges embarked on a fourteen-week training and orientation course organized by Liverpool Polytechnic School of Social Work with a major input from a multidisciplinary team including psychiatrists, psychologists, social workers, nurses and occupational therapists based at the Park Day Hospital. The training course enabled them to see themselves as counsellors as well as teachers. They subsequently offered support to mainstream further education staff as well as integrating students with mental health problems into college provision and running groups in a variety of outreach venues.

Within the psychiatric hospital in which I worked, where mental illness was the norm, patients referred to as having 'special needs' were the few who, because of severe behavioural excesses, age or frailty, were unable to live outside the institution even with twenty-four-hour care.

From a 'community' standpoint, however, the perspective is different, and all those people who have been institutionalized for any length of time have 'special needs' which require support. Within the college where I now work, for example, students with mental illness and/or behavioural problems which form a barrier to learning and often prevent them from using adult education provision without support are categorized as having 'special needs'.

The majority of hospitalized psychiatric patients are suffering from schizophrenia, a destructive mental illness which can be accompanied by delusions, olfactory, auditory and visual hallucinations and peculiar associations between objects. It may result in sufferers becoming 'socially disabled' (Richmond Fellowship, 1983) by an inability to make close personal relationships or to act independently and make decisions. The illness can be controlled by medication and may 'burn itself out' after a number of years, resulting in elderly people who are not ill, but who are so institutionalized that they are no longer able to live independently. Manic depressive illnesses, anxiety, obsessional states and personality disorders may all produce social disability. However, people who suffer from mental illnesses, although their thought processes may be disrupted, are not robbed of their intellect. While they do indeed have 'special needs' which have to be considered by the educationalist, it must also be remembered that the feelings experienced by people diagnosed as suffering from mental illness differ in *degree* rather than *kind* from feelings which we all experience.

In addition to a physical and emotional dependency on the institution as well as a lack of self-confidence and poor self-image, there are other factors connected with mental illness and institutionalization which affect learning. A poor concentration span may be a product of illness, effects of medication and institutionalization. Inconsistency of behaviour – for example, uncontrollable mood swings – may make systematic learning difficult and cause irregular attendance. Sufferers may find themselves unable to cope with an over-stimulating environment. It is particularly difficult to contend with other external stimuli or adapt to unexpected change if auditory hallucinations are being experienced; and the isolating nature of such illness makes it difficult to function within a group at the very time when group support would be most valuable.

The consequences of mental illness are such that sufferers may have to spend the rest of their lives avoiding undue pressure which could trigger another bout of illness. Following courses of study involving examinations may, therefore, be unrealistic. In any case, people who are newly resettled in the community are unlikely to have the confidence to enrol for educational provision, especially since they may have been actively discouraged from acting on their own initiative within the total institution.

My young son's exhortation to the rest of the family to be 'cool, calm and collective' in the face of a minor domestic crisis seems an appropriate expression to use to point out the importance of seeing the interests of the mentally ill collectively. This is essential at a time when the movement from institution to community care may well be accompanied by a movement from collectivity to the individual and thus from collective strength to the risk of marginalization and isolation.

While it would be unrealistic to make excessive claims for education in this context, it can and should involve processes which work towards recreating for the mentally ill a sense of belonging, purposefulness and dignity.

Lavender (1985) includes an account by an adult basic education tutor within a psychiatric unit attached to Castle House General Hospital. Her overall aim is 'to help adults to function better in society and to have access to information that controls their lives'. The point is made that only rarely can the learning interests and needs of the students in basic education be formed into a narrowly defined curriculum. Adult basic education for those who have been institutionalized has to include social skills, confidence building, communication and group skills in addition to literacy and numeracy work. Wiener (1986), for example, describes educational provision within a psychiatric day centre administered by Leeds Social Services Department. The curriculum includes, in addition to literacy and numeracy, social skills, preparation for employment, emotional development, craft activities, local history, current affairs and creative writing.

Clinically trained staff writing in paramedical journals also describe valuable day centre activities. At the Heatherwood Day Unit in East Berkshire (Vaughan and Prechner, 1985) activities are divided into specific therapies, creative arts and crafts, social activities and rehabilitation. 'Remedial education' appears in the final category, following 'cooking, shopping, personal care'! Similarly, 'education' appears at the bottom of the list of twelve activities (including creativity development, welfare rights, medication advice) provided at the Kirkdale Resource Centre in London (Bumstead, 1985). While the categories employed illustrate the different viewpoints of professionals from different disciplines, it would seem to me that *all* the activities listed must fulfil educational aims consistent with the project's concept of allowing its clients 'to develop in an environment which encourages them to take responsibility for their own lives'.

I would agree with Wiener (1986) that

> the whole experience of being in the centre is a continuing education experience. People are developing social and decision-making skills and learning about themselves and the world around them.

All of the provision referred to so far, however, takes place in discrete groups in day centres where the students are separated from other groups. It is true that

> extending boundaries to encompass a wider range of ability and disability – to welcome as 'normal' what had previously been excluded as 'different' – is no easy matter: society's sense of wholeness is put into jeopardy.
>
> (Donovan, 1985)

For this reason, separate groups may well be the right first step from institution to community. However, I do feel that this kind of provision should be seen as a bridge which eventually affords access to mainstream educational provision and enables people to move on.

The identification of appropriate mainstream provision needs to be undertaken in conjunction with a tutor who has responsibility for students with mental health problems and who can offer counselling and guidance. For example, students can be channelled towards courses which lead to qualifications through continuous assessment rather than examination. Moreover, volunteers can be drawn upon to act as 'co-students' to offer support in mainstream classes. This cannot, however, happen overnight, since relationships need time to develop and confidence in the 'co-educator' needs to grow. It is for this reason that we are currently running a volunteer training course in conjunction with the voluntary services organizer at Bolton General Hospital Adult Mental Health Sub-unit. It is intended that the volunteers, many of whom are already working in day and drop-in centres throughout Bolton, will learn about the provision which the college offers and will subsequently accompany day centre users to college and give them support within the classes.

In addition to these informal networks a second, more formal, network needs to be created to bring together the different agencies and professions which are involved in community care of the mentally ill – principally education, health, social services and voluntary agencies – in order to maximize resources, promote greater understanding of each other's aims and to increase knowledge among education practitioners and the wider community about the nature of mental illness. In my experience, such networks tend to develop on an *ad hoc* basis, and I believe that there is a need to promote more systematic forms of inter-agency liaison and collaboration.

Straightening the bend

Many of the mentally ill people with whom I have worked have desperately unhappy memories of their previous educational experiences. Indeed, they are not alone in this, since for many adults, school days were far from being the happiest days of their lives. The experiences of people suffering from mental illness seem both to reflect and to magnify those of other people. Many of them have also experienced life in an authoritarian institutional environment, separated and alienated from the wider community, upon which their own personalities and identities have made little or no impact.

Moving patients from the institution to the community is easy – as the now famous comment of the Social Services Committee Report of 1985 implies: 'Any fool can close a hospital.' Yet 'straightening the bend' by bringing the mentally ill back into the main arena of community life is much more complex. It has the following implications which reach well beyond the patients and professionals of the institutional community to the members of the wider external community:

1. Within the institution, mental illness is the norm; it is condoned and, indeed, expected. There is a need for far greater awareness outside hospitals and a dispelling of the terrible stigma which is still attached to those who have been labelled 'mentally ill'.
2. Life at home with their families can be more barren for sufferers than life within the institution. There is a tendency for families of schizophrenia sufferers in particular to withdraw from social networks. There is a need for active support for carers in the community.
3. Within the institution, the mentally ill have priority; no one is vying with them for resources. In the wider community, however, it is all too easy for others to have a larger share of the cake – others who have louder voices and more power. There is a need for the collective voice of people with mental illness to be heard. Individual integration into the community can easily result in fragmentation and the consequent disappearance of the needs of the mentally ill from the political agenda.

4. Within the institution, professionals have clearly defined roles. The move to the community brings with it a blurring of those roles and a feeling of being under threat from other disciplines and services. It is vital that channels are provided to facilitate successful multidisciplinary work within the community.

It seems to me that education has a key part to play in each of these areas. All educational attempts at 'straightening the bend' should include awareness-raising, multidisciplinary staff development and support for carers in addition to a broad curriculum and educational counselling designed to enable a marginalized group of people to make their own voices heard and exercise more control over their lives. Finally, it must be emphasized that community care is far from being a cheap option. It is essential that resources are available to ensure that it can become a way of restoring dignity and justice to people who have been shut away and forgotten about for far too long.

REFERENCES

Bumstead, C. (1985) 'The Kirkdale Resource Centre: a new model of community adult mental health care'. *British Journal of Occupational Therapy*, **48**(1) (October), 305–6.

Department of Health and Social Security (1981) *Care in Action*. London: HMSO.

Donovan, J. (ed.) (1985) *Experiences of a Changing Kind: Adult Education in Psychiatric Hospitals and Day Centres*. MIND in association with WEA Yorkshire North District.

Foster, L. (1988) 'Writers' workshops, the word processor and the psychiatric patient'. *British Journal of Occupational Therapy*, **51**(6) (June), 191–2.

Freire, P. (1972) *Cultural Action for Freedom*. Harmondsworth: Penguin.

Freire, P. (1987) *Reading the Word and the World*. London: Routledge & Kegan Paul.

Goffman, E. (1968) *Asylums*. Harmondsworth: Penguin.

Griffiths, R. (1988) *Community Care: Agenda for Action*. London: HMSO.

Hargreaves, D. (1982) *The Challenge of the Comprehensive School*. London: Routledge & Kegan Paul.

King's Fund (1988) *Collaboration for Change*. London: King's Fund Centre.

Lavender, P. (1985) 'Singer and listener: basic education work with the mentally ill'. *Viewpoints*, **2**, ALBSU (February), 5–10.

Martin, I. (1987) 'Community education: towards a theoretical analysis'. In G. Allen, J. Bastiani, I. Martin and K. Richards (eds) *Community Education: An Agenda for Education Reform*. Milton Keynes: Open University Press.

Ministry of Health (1962) *The Hospital Plan for England and Wales*. London: HMSO.

Ministry of Health (1963) *Health and Welfare: The Development of Community Care*. London: HMSO.

Ministry of Health (1989) *Caring for People*. London: HMSO.

Richmond Fellowship (1983) *Mental Health and the Community Report of the Richmond Fellowship Enquiry*. Winchester: Richmond Fellowship Press.

Roberts, K. (1987) 'Another island in the crowd . . . access to education and training for clients of psychiatric hospitals and day centres in Liverpool'. *Educare*, **29** (November), 19–23.

Social Services Committee (1985) *Community Care with Special Reference to Adult Mentally Ill and Mentally Handicapped People*. London: HMSO.

Vaughan, P. J. and Prechner, M. (1985) 'Occupation or therapy in psychiatric day care?'. *British Journal of Occupational Therapy*, **48**(6) (June), 169–71.

Walker, A. (1983) 'A caring community'. In H. Glennerster (ed.) *The Future of the Welfare State*. London: Heinemann.

Webb, B. (1975) *Minds in Touch*. London: Epworth Press.

Wiener, R. (1986) 'Adult education in a psychiatric day centre'. *Adult Education*, **59**(2) (September), 128–33.

Chapter 9

Community Development and 'Customer Care': Conflict or Convergence?

Sue Charteris

The restructuring of local government poses critical challenges to those responsible for the provision of educational and social services. The logic of central government policy is to redefine accountability and effectiveness in market terms, i.e. as a response to individual demand rather than collective need. Sue Charteris, drawing upon experience at both grass-roots and strategic levels within local government, suggests that the apparent value conflict between new-fangled 'customer care' and old-fashioned 'community development' can be managed equitably as well as efficiently if pragmatism is tempered by principle. Within the unintended outcomes of centrally imposed change lie significant opportunities – as well as threats. In particular, there is now an unprecedented opportunity to demarginalize community development and bring it to the centre of a socially redistributive and democratic strategy for the management of change. This is the basic challenge of the politics of practice for local government today.

INTRODUCTION

Community development initiatives involving local authorities have for years remained peripheral to mainstream thinking on the provision of local authority services. Community action has been tolerated at best, an irritant at worst, in its endeavours to press a complacent bureaucracy into becoming more responsive to the needs of local communities. Yet there is now a surprising resurgence of interest in community development approaches in local government just at a time when central government legislation is challenging the very survival of 'providing institutions' as we know them. Local authorities are being bombarded with advice on how to be more accountable to their users. 'Put people first, listen to your customers, and be more responsive to their needs', says the local government watchdog, the Audit Commission (1988) – not at first sight the likeliest of bodies to spring to the defence of local communities. And local authorities are listening. Having become increasingly conscious of their remoteness, they are urgently seeking ways of getting closer to local residents.

'CUSTOMER CARE' AND LOCAL AUTHORITIES

Work on developing 'customer care strategies' has become high fashion in local government, with a new language to match, borrowed largely from the private sector. This reawakening of interest in the consumer may offer opportunities to develop new approaches to service delivery; but first it is necessary to unpack what is being said and by whom, for there are dangers within the opportunities. If it is the customer who matters now, what has happened to the client, the user, resident, ratepayer, consumer and citizen? Are customers merely a multiplicity of individuals, or are there still collective needs that cannot be addressed in the language of the marketplace?

My interest in these questions stems from several years' experience as a worker on a local community action project followed by Town Hall work on strategic planning and policy development. One of my central aims has been to help to bridge the gap that frequently exists between the formal adoption of local authority policies and local communities' own appraisals of their needs. The difficulties can be considerable, for very clear communication channels and a willingness to use them are needed if the views of local residents are to be taken into account in time to affect decision making.

It is, therefore, refreshing to see 'edicts' on customer care emerging from official bodies and mainstream local government journals because they offer a way into the debate about how local authorities provide services and for whom. This issue has never been more crucial because local authorities, in having to adapt their structures and systems to compete with the private sector, are in danger of forgetting to ask themselves whether the market-led model is actually transferable or appropriate to public sector local government.

This question can be explored by comparing the strategies offered by customer care with community development principles, the former being based on meeting individual demand for a product, the latter being about collective definitions of need. As Robin Hambleton suggests in *Consumerism, Decentralisation and Democracy* (1988), 'there is a major risk that many authorities will attempt to implement some or all of these new ideas . . . all of which share the broad aim of closing the them and us gap . . . without thinking through the implications'.

In this chapter I intend to examine the pressures on local government to change and ask whether the various prescriptions on offer, in particular customer care initiatives, can be used to promote community development strategies more systematically in the day-to-day provision of services.

Although rationales may differ, there is a shared recognition among those offering new 'ways forward' that local authorities have become increasingly remote from local residents. One major indicator is the voting level at local elections. The 1986 local elections, for instance, produced a turnout of 39.3 per cent in metropolitan districts and 45.4 per cent in the London boroughs (Stewart and Stoker, 1988). National consumer surveys (AMA, 1988) show that, although local government is quite well regarded, there is still considerable public ignorance of what services local councils, as distinct from central government or health authorities, actually provide.

Perhaps it is not surprising, therefore, that, until the recent spate of legislative reform, there was little challenge to local councils' right to be the sole providers of public housing, state education and a variety of social and amenity services. In fact, during the 1980s authorities extended their traditional remit quite considerably. Many local authorities, for example, followed the example of the former Greater London Council and created new structures to implement proactive policies on equal opportunities, economic development and welfare rights as well as developmental strategies on issues such as community-based child care.

But the task of running increasingly complex institutions, hampered by tightening constraints on public sector spending, has so preoccupied officers and elected members alike that most authorities have become increasingly inward-looking and defensive. Although innovative, community-based practice has developed, it is generally peripheral to the overriding concern to 'manage' the affairs of the authority. Even among those local authorities which have developed new forms of organization, such as decentralization initiatives, there are very few examples of significant devolution of power to local neighbourhoods. Some councils have established neighbourhood committees to work alongside decentralized local offices but few have moved to what Hambleton and Hoggett (1988) identify as the logical next step, the 'democratisation of local services'. The delegation of budgets to local area committees, composed predominantly of residents with local ward councillors in a minority, raises fundamental political and procedural issues for local authorities. In Newcastle's Priority Areas, for example, each of which has an annual budget of £40 000, decisions to spend over £500 have to be ratified by a council committee (Hambleton and Hoggett, 1988). While these procedures seem to local councils to be sensible safeguards, they also limit local residents' confidence that such local forums have teeth.

Ironically, the strongest pressure on local councils to rethink has emanated from central government's legislative reforms, particularly the Education Reform Act 1988 and the Local Government and Housing Act 1988. The latter, for example, obliges local authorities to put key services out to competitive tender as well as substantially changing the way public housing provision is organized and funded. The motivation behind the government's combined initiatives is perceived within local government as being quite clearly to reduce the role of local authorities to that of 'enabling agencies' whose main function is to oversee contracts.

Certainly these reforms, challenging the very basis of local government, have shaken local authorities out of any remaining complacency. What both community activists and central government have in common is a belief that local councils which remain unresponsive do not deserve to exist.

The community development critique of local government challenges the bureaucratic top-down model of planning and provision and its untested assumptions about what is good for the people. Community development philosophies support an enabling model of provision, albeit from a totally different premise to that of central government, i.e. that local authorities should be exploring ways of stimulating and empowering local people to articulate their interests and needs and work towards solutions on a collective rather than an individual basis. This may inevitably mean that communities will from time to time come into conflict with their local authority.

As a process, community development needs to have as its starting point a recognition that inequality and discrimination exist in the ways that services are allocated. A central objective is, therefore, to facilitate communities, attempt to redress imbalances, and obtain more direct and equal access to services. This approach does not question the right of local authorities to provide services, but it does call for greater flexibility and more attention to the appropriateness of services to meet differing needs.

The Association of Metropolitan Authorities (AMA, 1988) argues that councils are bad at communicating with their electorates. They have been reluctant to embark on consultation exercises (often questioning their validity) and should be doing much more to involve local residents in decisions that affect their lives rather than imposing 'expert' solutions from on high. The AMA goes on to suggest that local authorities consider much more seriously than in the past the role that community development can play in the process of achieving greater accountability and effectiveness.

The strength of the AMA paper is that it suggests a prominent role for community development strategies in achieving other policy objectives which councils may consider more pressing. There is considerable academic literature on the philosophy of community development, but the AMA, instead of rehearsing all this, simply places community development at the heart of the local government function in the contemporary political context. It argues a role for community development in tackling discrimination, for example, and ensuring that equal opportunities strategies are effectively implemented as well as work on performance review strategies. It proposes that community development can facilitate inter-agency co-ordination, inform debates on the quality and prioritization of services, and promote more systematic dialogue with the voluntary sector.

The other current critique I wish to explore is that issuing from the Audit Commission. This was established in 1982 to increase the financial accountability of local authorities and to protect the interests of ratepayers. Its primarily policing role caused councillors and trade unions to regard its findings with suspicion. In their view, the prevailing emphasis on finance-led indicators for measuring local authority performance distorted and over-simplified the role of local government. Latterly, however, the Commission seems to have become more sympathetic towards the object of its scrutiny.

In its management paper *The Competitive Council* (1988) the Commission reminds local authorities that 'people no longer accept that the council knows best'. The Commission starts from a premise totally different from that of the AMA, i.e. that quality rather than quantity should be the main target, and that 'customers' will go elsewhere if the quality of service is not high enough. Like the AMA paper, however, the Commission urges local authorities to understand their 'customers' better, to find out what they want and to plan accordingly. The Commission even uses some of the same arguments as the AMA, for example on the need to stimulate local democracy. It argues that services need to become more 'user friendly', that authorities should find ways of improving dialogue not only with local businesses but also community groups and of facilitating upward communication, using the knowledge and experience of front-line staff to plan service development. Ironically perhaps, the Audit Commission has in some ways turned out to be the unexpected – and powerful – ally of those in local government who have been arguing the case for community development principles and strategies in the face of the pervasive 'business as usual' culture.

DISCOVERING THE CUSTOMER

Many authorities, borrowing initiatives from private sector organizations on 'customer service orientation', are developing ways of 'getting closer to the public' (Local

Government Training Board, 1987). These 'customer care' programmes have several common features:

- reviewing performance, developing targets and being open with the public about the levels of service the council aims to provide;
- developing procedures for dealing with complaints quickly;
- allowing people more 'choice' in the type of service they receive;
- listening and obtaining the views of local residents;
- consulting with service users; and
- training reception and telephone staff to see problems presented to them from the consumer's point of view.

Choices for whom?

There is, however, a fundamental problem to overcome if such strategies are to be implemented equitably. Rarely within the customer care literature is the customer explicitly defined. But one thing is clear: the customer is an individual, and there is an assumption that individual customers have identical needs and will buy the same product if the quality and the price are attractive. This then is a marketplace definition of choice. In reality, however, local authorities provide a whole range of services to people with quite different needs. While inadequate resources may mean that not everyone who 'needs' a home help can get one, they go to those whom councils decide are the 'most needy'. What is more, we must not lose sight of the fact that not all residents are voluntarily consumers of local authority services. Few people, for example, would choose bed and breakfast accommodation if other housing was available to them. We should, therefore, be wary of using the word 'customer' interchangeably with 'client'.

Local authorities, as local government, have to find ways of determining how to allocate scarce resources as fairly as possible to the community as a whole. One way forward is for them to involve their residents in a more effective dialogue about how these collective choices are made. It is also important that performance review is informed not only by the Audit Commission's three E's of Economy, Effectiveness and Efficiency but also the fourth E of Equity: Who is using the services? Are they relevant to their needs? Whom are we failing to reach? In this way, it is possible to combine the requirements placed on local authorities by central government and auditors and at the same time to involve community groups in a dialogue about performance review. Having prioritized objectives clearly, councils should be able to create ways in which local communities of interest and need can help to evaluate and improve services.

The limits of consultation

Perhaps local authorities of all political persuasions have been attracted to the ideas of customer care partly because of their reservations about consultation through group-based networks. Gyford (1987) summarizes the arguments well. Politicians are often dubious about the representativeness of community forums, and community 'leaders' in particular. They see such forums as dominated by professional 'activists' with no apparent grassroots support. Furthermore, there are legitimate fears that consultation with particular interest groups may exclude the public at large. There is often concern that if such forums are unrepresentative they will undermine equal opportunities objectives, or that if such groups make excessive demands the authority will be embarrassed in having to say no. This may explain why the politics of consulting individuals rather than groups or networks of interest within localities may at first seem attractive. But nowhere in the consumer rights model is there sufficient explanation of how this can be achieved effectively in a public sector context.

So the question arises; *how* do you obtain the views of those with as yet unarticulated *needs* if the authority is not already in touch with them? This is where the private sector approach begins to break down because it does not address the concept of social need at all. Advertisers' assumptions in marketing a product are that there is no point in trying to reach potential customers who cannot afford to pay: consequently the advertising strategy would be to ignore them. Customer surveys are not sophisticated or discriminating enough to obtain the views of indirect users of provision, such as the families of beneficiaries of a meals-on-wheels service, and involve wider social and economic benefits than the services offered directly to the individual. Consumer surveys are useful only if they can be used to obtain and analyse data and then develop a dialogue between collective views about how existing services could be improved and future services planned. How often do the results of consumer surveys get fed back to respondents so that such a dialogue could develop?

As councils begin to consult their customers in new ways, it is likely that the skills of community development workers as 'facilitators of change' will gain greater recognition and respect. Change is now inevitable. There is no prospect of local authorities being stable organizations in the foreseeable future, and managers must manage in an atmosphere of uncertainty. Tom Peters's handbook *Thriving on Chaos* (1988), which advises on techniques for 'creating total customer responsiveness', would have been considered bizarre reading for local government managers only a few years ago. Now it is a standard text. Peters, in his introduction, stresses that: 'The leadership prescriptions essentially address only two questions. First, "How do you induce people to love change as much as they've hated it in the past?" and then, "How do you lead/guide/control what looks like anarchy by normal standards?"'

So how can local authorities afford not to be without effective community development strategies? The AMA is convinced that they cannot, and recommends the establishment of permanent community development units. Care, however, must be taken not to institutionalize community development. Such work in local authorities has to remain accountable at all stages to the communities it is intended to serve. Community development also offers a way of helping councils to target resources to those most in need – as distinct from those who make the loudest noise – and to cut across the competing interests of departmentalism. Community development can help to ensure the achievement all four E's.

As might be expected though, there is a sting in the tail. Just at a time when community development has been gaining wider acceptance, new constraints have been placed on local government workers engaged in it. For example, it has often been the practice of community workers to stimulate grassroots activity around specific local issues. However, the restrictions on council employees' involvement in 'political' activity introduced in recent legislation must be regarded as a major constraint on the community development process, as is the general cash crisis in local government.

A NEW PARTNERSHIP

Despite these reservations, I am convinced that community development has an unprecedented opportunity to influence the way in which local authorities operate. Community development should now be at the heart of local government, as Stewart and Stoker (1988) imply when they redefine local government as 'community government', i.e. government which involves the governed and recognizes or rediscovers that it is 'the government of difference with a concern for the community beyond the provision of services to individuals'. According to Blunkett and Straw (1988), community development is the process that can bridge the gap between consumption and citizenship: 'We are none of us merely consumers, we are consumers and citizens, citizens and electors, electors and tax payers, tax payers and contributors, contributors and producers. Such a complex of relationships is the community, it is something greater than the sum total of consumers'.

As we move further into the 1990s, community development may be the way local authorities can rebuild a dialogue with local residents, thus ensuring that the demands of the customer can be reconciled with the needs and rights of those whose voice is seldom heard in the marketplace.

REFERENCES

Association of Metropolitan Authorities (1988) *Community Development Policy Guidelines*. London: AMA.

Audit Commission (1988) *The Competitive Council*. London: Audit Commission for England and Wales.

Blunkett, D. and Straw, J. (1988) *Consumers and the Community*. Labour Policy Review Group. London: Labour Party.

Gyford, G. (1987) 'Decentralization within authorities', in M. Parkinson (ed.) *Reshaping Local Government*. Newbury: Policy Journals.

Hambleton, R. (1988) *Consumerism, Decentralisation and Democracy*. School for Advanced Urban Studies, University of Bristol.

Hambleton, R. and Hoggett, P. (eds) (1988) *Decentralization and Democracy*. School for Advanced Studies, University of Bristol.

Local Government Training Board (1987) *Getting Closer to the Public*. Luton: LGTB Publications.

Peters, T. (1988) *Thriving on Chaos*. London: Macmillan.

Stewart, J. and Stoker, G. (1988) *From Administration to Local Community Government*. London: Fabian Society.

Chapter 10

Networking: Tactics of Survival

Pam Flynn

Drawing upon her extensive experience as an activist in a variety of community-based social movements, Pam Flynn argues that the real site of struggle has moved from the formalized politics of institutions to the informal politics of oppositional networking. This is a relatively fluid and unpredictable process, loose and shifting alliances being formed around specific issues. What is most significant about such explicitly counter-hegemonic activity is the sense of confidence and solidarity participants gain from it and the links it forges in ordinary people's experience between the personal and the political. Networking is an educative process as well as a strategy of resistance, 'with women as its principal protagonists', which shows how the vision of an alternative future can be nurtured within a 'macro' context that is both economically and ideologically reductionist. As such, Flynn believes that networking, as both a way of working and a statement of alternative values, can help to sow the seeds of a genuine liberation.

INTRODUCTION

The first part of this chapter shows how networking within women's education, the wider women's movement and other campaigning groups offers a mechanism for empowerment, even survival, in the present climate of economic and ideological reductionism. By 'empowerment' is meant the imparting of power to do things and gaining the confidence to feel powerful. Empowerment is both internal and psychological and external, action-orientated and oppositional. By 'reductionism' is meant the process of narrowing down our understanding of the nature of the economy, the workforce, people's culture and opportunities. Again, the process can be seen as both internal and external. Internally, reductionism is shown as a limiting of perception. People feel hopeless about the future and lack belief in their capacity to achieve their aspirations. Externally, reductionism manifests itself in the 'balance sheet' mentality, which for example reduces local education and health services to local budgets controlled by school governors and GPs. Reductionism is also characterized by double-speak. Public services become businesses to be marketed.

This chapter draws upon experience gained in the north-east of England in a variety of local projects and in trade unions. It then goes on to look at the campaign against

Clause 28 of the Local Government Act 1988, which forbids local authorities to 'promote' homosexuality and, in this context, at Noel Greig's play *Plague of Innocence*, which was taken on tour in Sheffield and South Yorkshire by the Crucible Theatre in Education team in early 1988. The teachers' pack for this play formed an important element of support, particularly in terms of curriculum, for the networking practice of educationalists opposed to Clause 28 as well as the AIDS panic and the wider attack on working people.

A VIEW OF POLITICS NOW

The 1980s may well be viewed by future historians as a lost decade. They will certainly be able to point to a strategic assault by the Thatcher government on both the infrastructure and the superstructure of liberal social democracy. Assaults on the industrial base – coal, water, steel, electricity, shipbuilding, engineering, research and development – have been accompanied by assaults on education at all levels, from preschool to higher education.

Alongside these assaults has been a dismantling of services built partly as a direct result of working people's agitation and struggle: the NHS, the social security system, pensions, school meals, public transport, child benefit and trade union rights (Keys *et al.*, 1983). To complement this process of deconstruction there has been a crude attempt to mould a new morality based on a combination of self-interest and moral panic.

In the face of these assaults, the trade union movement, the traditional organizational form of social advance for working people, has been outmanoeuvred. Trade union struggle has become more defensive than ever. The sociology of the workforce has changed in the last decade. Workers in Britain, and internationally, have become fragmented and cannot be mobilized in huge collective aggregations. Increasingly, workers see themselves as individual consumers in the marketplace. Mao Tse-Tung's (1968) analysis is apposite here:

> In social struggle, the forces representing the advanced class sometimes suffer defeat, not because their ideas are incorrect but because in the balance of forces engaged in struggle they are not as powerful for the time being as the forces of reaction; they are, therefore, temporarily defeated, but they are bound to triumph sooner or later.

Mao offers us the longer view. And by standing back, it is possible to discern other forms and levels of oppositional activity.

A finer view: making our future

> There is no such thing as too many people communicating good ideas and working to bring about change.
>
> (Neitlich, 1985)

> If you want to understand what's happening in British society, you could do no better than to look at women. They're at the receiving end of much of what's happening. They're also the people trying to change their lives.
>
> (Bowman, 1987)

At the 'micro' level surges of activity are evident which contribute to political opposition and in many ways offer a pointer to a better future. Examples are: Network, Women and Training North East (WATNE); the Working with Girls Development Group; North East Women's Self Defence Group; East End Women's Activities Group, as well as Rape Crisis and Incest Survivor groups and a number of Women's Aid refuges.

What is it about the style of work of such groups that constitutes an 'alternative'? I believe that it is their general ethos of optimism about the possibility of change and, in particular, their commitment to networking as a way of working that is consonant with their values and purposes.

NETWORKING

Networking is a powerful process. One of its more publicly acknowledged examples in the 1980s was the Greenham Common peace camp, a camp for women, which touched the minds, spirits and actions of millions of women and men worldwide.

For me, networking is essentially the maintenance of an open, rather than a closed, information system for ideas and action which has its roots in respect for persons. On an individual level, it means that something I have, or someone I know, or a perspective that I have, is shared as widely as possible and whenever possible. Beyond this, networking begins with the proposition that each person carries a unique experience deserving of respect. Individuals have many skills and much information, frequently underrated. Networking shares and develops these skills, information and perspectives in a supportive framework. The activities of women, black people, peace activists, lesbians and gay men, anti-fascist activists, tenants' and community groups form an additional line of resistance in favour of liberation. Obviously these groups and interests include many who are members of more than one constituency as well as trade union, Labour Party and other political party members.

These groupings of activists offer a model of collective endeavour which contrasts with much that is visible in traditional working-class organizations. As an active trade unionist, I have frequently become exhausted and frustrated at the sheer alienation and confusion that traditional trade union structures and procedures can engender in women and men lay members. Systems devised for the ordered and protected running of organizations born in illegal conspiracy have become distorted so that models designed for democratic centralism and security are today meaningless to many members. Rigid and entrenched structures of formal organization can stifle creative action.

In the north-east of England many community-based projects are beginning to demonstrate an alternative style of working. Focusing on those working with women, it is possible to list some examples: Saheli (a support and campaign group for black women workers), the Bridge Women's Education Project in Washington, Tyneside Women's Employment Project, three women's community health projects in Newcastle/Gateshead, Breakthrough (the North East Women Returners). Within any particular project or activity networking operates so that a person's thinking is valued, leading to a sense of autonomy, powerfulness and confidence. Skills owned by one become potential common property, the skills sharing sometimes being facilitated by the design and running of the project (e.g. see NIACE, 1987).

The networking process links individuals together in a recognition that skills, knowledge and activity can be shared, be it in festival, demonstration, conference, activism or educational process. Far from believing that a focus on individual rights and personal development is bourgeois or reactionary, I would argue that for the individual to be valued as powerful contributes to an optimistic sense of self and that this self-value is a basic building block in the empowerment of the larger collective, a building block in the networking process.

As an example, women's health projects on Tyneside consistently emphasize that mental health is part of overall health. They also seek to make it clear that health is conditioned by factors such as poverty and the quality and accessibility of housing and public services. Women in health groups have met to devise ways of eating healthily on a low budget and have undertaken together a range of outdoor activities that might be denied to them individually through lack of confidence, finance or opportunity. Women's health groups have linked with tenants' organizations to campaign on housing policy and with neighbourhood learning groups and community work training groups. Alliances are not always obvious, but links are discernible, for example, between local community health groups, tenants, trade unionists and black groups. Women are the primary activists in most of these organizations: their activism is both internal and external. Hilary Armstrong (1986) comments on this process:

> Feminism has enabled us to link those things that have always been regarded as private and personal to what is going on in state institutions, to political and economic life . . . When I've talked to past women students . . . their overriding impression is of going through enormous personal change, while other people in the family watched with bewilderment . . . Most women have continued to live with their families in their working-class neighbourhoods, but with an understanding of what is going on in that neighbourhood, and in the lives of their friends, that is clearly reflected in the sort of work they are now able to do.

A good example of the process of networking is offered by the campaign for childcare within continuing and further or higher education. Good practice and breakthroughs in one area have been widely shared and built upon elsewhere. Crèches are still far from commonplace in educational establishments in the North East (are they commonplace anywhere?), but the insistence on good childcare by projects such as Bridge, Tyneside Women's Health Project and Tyneside Women's Employment Project (TWEP) has led to significant breakthroughs in Newcastle, Gateshead and South Tyneside.

Childcare has become a policy objective of students, users and staff alike in many organizations. In July 1987, TWEP convened an important Crèche Charter Day in Newcastle which was attended by crèche users, crèche staff and local authority policy makers as well as crèche providers. Since then, the Charter of Crèches has been taken up in a variety of networks, linking the North East with London through the activities of the Crèche Campaign Information Group on Tyneside and the Childcare Now campaign nationally.

Alicia Bruce's experience in community-based women's education in Scotland enables her to suggest how social change and personal change are inter-related (see Flynn *et al.*, 1986):

> Women's education is not static, but continually active, incorporating and adjusting. This allows the opportunity of change through variation. The theory and practice of education and action for change can, therefore, undermine oppressive structures, through the development of active and critical politics. The growth of educational networks with alternative

values is being increasingly recognised as an important way forward for subordinate groups.

Bruce's case study of Ann is a microcosm of this process, especially as it relates to women trade unionists. Ann, who was employed as a domestic auxiliary in a hospital, joined an informal adult education group after contact with an existing participant. She then joined a Refresher English group and related her work to minutes, agendas, letter-writing and grammar. Over a period of months, she gained confidence, developed social contacts, shared her skills and experience and began to analyse problems in her work situation. She stood and was elected as a shop steward at work and subsequently developed her learning about women in the trade union movement, socialism, economic theory and welfare rights. Finally, all the women in her study group stood alongside Ann on the picket line during the health workers' dispute. Ann's trade union was influenced to begin to break down traditional male domination. Thus, co-operative learning and networking, starting with Ann the individual and building from there, led to the development of critical theory and oppositional practice which challenged the dominant patriarchy. A similar process is also documented in the stories of Connie and Mary, tenant activists in the North East, whose informal learning and co-operative networking led them to develop an active critique of both the local state and of national housing policy (see Flynn *et al.*, 1986). Margaret Marshall and Eileen Aird have written in detail about the personal empowerment arising from involvement in feminist-centred non-formal education (Marshall, 1985; Aird, 1985).

Judy Seymour has also written, in the context of working with girls, of the relation-ship between acknowledging personal change and liberation and its connection with optimistic social change (see Flynn *et al.*, 1986):

> We must find our own relationship with the oppression so that we know what to fight for. We must know when, and how, to facilitate someone else to fight for it. Above all, the changes we are seeking will happen through affirmative, optimistic action, not through negative reaction.

From the personal agendas of individual women of all ages, in particular the general desire for validation and confidence, come the recognition of and the assertion of responsibility and powerfulness. When translated into action and shared, the resulting co-operative, open style of operation and campaigning for change contributes to the defeat of patterns of powerlessness and competition between individuals and groups.

A process with its foundation in interpersonal relationships, networking enables the building of close, trusting and respectful relations. The effective communication within and between projects and campaigns which results is different from, and freer than, much of the competitive, closed and rigid communication elsewhere. Isolation on a personal and group level is combated, producing a real sense of unity of purpose which is often borne out in united action. In terms of resistance to attack, networking offers an optimistic framework. Progress is quickly shared on a variety of levels so that it is consolidated and built upon elsewhere. There is a standing of ground, a refusal to give up and even a determination to gain new and additional resources.

Networking and Clause 28

On 2 February 1988 Rachel Cox and two other women abseiled into the House of Lords as a protest against the then Clause 28 of the Local Government Bill. Rachel had lived at Greenham Common for eighteen months and draws a connection between the protests against the Clause and protests against Cruise missiles (Cox, 1988):

> Greenham was a women's challenge to male ordered structures. It was the best finishing school in the world. It produced thousands of trained activists skilled in . . . actions and it was that experience that gave me the nerve to slide down a washing line in the House of Lords . . . The Civil Rights nature of the issue unites gays and lesbians with many other people . . . in the long term thousands of us will be politicized. This will be a good thing for all of us, because such a can of worms will be opened up that the powers that be may very well wish that they'd left things as they were.

Rachel Cox and her colleagues took the networking tactics of Greenham Common into the struggle against the clause. Their actions were just part of a whole range of activity culminating in massive turnouts on demonstrations, marches and rallies against it. Though subsequently translated into law, the government's crude attempt to legislate against life-style proved unworkable. No one has yet dared to test the clause in the courts. Apparent failure to stop the legislation conceals real gains in terms of lesbians' and gay men's increased consciousness, confidence, pride and solidarity.

Networking, AIDS and theatre in education

Noel Greig's theatre in education jazz play/symphony for voices *Plague of Innocence* toured schools and youth clubs in Sheffield, South Yorkshire and Derbyshire in early 1988. It had been commissioned as part of the Crucible Theatre's programme of work on gender and sexuality.

The play, despite glowing reviews, in no way preached solely to the converted. Its performance in schools was pilloried by the local press and its director was subjected to abusive telephone calls and letters. Negotiation of performances was carefully carried out with school governors, parents and teachers. In the end, its educative and transformative impact upon the young people who saw it and worked with its teaching pack, and upon teachers and trainers, became evident. The play won the British Theatre Association Drama Review Award of 1988.

The characters in the play are all 'potentials', banished to The Gladelands, as plague carriers. People with HIV/AIDS initially, and later anyone 'potentially' a threat to the state, are banished to live separately and apart from the residents of the Primocities. The play deals movingly, crisply and effectively with the transference from victim to villain. Its simple language and short lines hold complex ideas. According to Sheffield Crucible Theatre in Education (1988), the play does not only deal with HIV, but looks at a whole world where racism, power, prejudice, HIV and AIDS and inequality are all interconnected. The play looks at the way issues like HIV and AIDS cannot be separated from the concepts of power and prejudice, and tries to make the connections.

The five characters in the play all go through a transition from a period of helplessness to a period of change, when they make a stand for what they believe in and fight against a system which discriminates.

Here are three short sequences from Greig's (unpublished) play*:

thin cotton,
dirty green,
number printed on the sleeve,
bright red patch
above the heart,
three letters in black
HIV.

And so a new word floated down
from Whitehall,
entered the hearts, the minds,
of the English
Promoter
Definition
To promote:
To encourage the development of

And all the while
the decrees,
more and more,
floating down from the sky
like snow, like sleet
Potential.

Plague of Innocence is an example of how a creative and imaginative work, taken up by performers and toured widely, can become a tool of opposition by virtue of the fact that it stands for integrity, for questioning, for truth and affirmation of identity. Set at the millennium, the play looks forward and back as well as at the present. In breaking the silence, it contributes to an open information system. It stands for opposition and resistance, and thus has a place in the educational networking process.

Oppositional networking in Newcastle

In March 1984, in response to Newcastle City Council's freeze of jobs and services, rises in rents and rates (all forced by the withdrawal by the government of rate support grant) an *ad hoc* organization rooted in the trade union movement, Newcastle Public Services Alliance, drew up the 'Defend Newcastle Charter'. Activity around the Charter linked seventeen trade unions, the Unemployed Workers' Movement, the Labour Party at ward level, play schemes, tenants' associations, the WEA, a community law project, the school meals service, the direct labour organization of the Council and a variety of community work projects.

Soon the rate-capped authority was forced to cut jobs and services, and this trend has continued. Yet within Newcastle community life is still vibrant and the links are still being made. Those involved in children's play, tenants' groups, community associa-

Plague of Innocence copyright © 1989 by Noel Greig. By permission of Michael Imison Playwrights Ltd, 28 Almeida Street, London N1 1TD.

tions, youth clubs, arts and theatre groups and women's groups are still reached by those trade unionists within the city who can see the importance of standing for a service – as well as for a job or a wage. Today the picture is, if anything, richer because the networks of communication have widened to include black groups, gay and lesbian groups and groups working on the issue of HIV/AIDS.

Attacks by central government have engendered new forms of resistance and opposition as well as new alliances. Projects currently engaged in affirmative work link women's employment and health issues to anti-racist and anti-fascist practice. Black women's groups link with neighbourhood learning centres which in turn link with peace workers and trade unionists. For all these many projects and individuals, the process of networking, of sharing and communication, is fundamentally oppositional. Such opposition works on a number of levels: opposition to the national political culture of reductionism, to the local state's response, to uncaring bureaucracy and hidebound tradition, to moral panic and to orthodoxy and alienation.

The articulation of the need for services and the demand for resources are in direct contradiction to local and national reductionism and take on the character of political opposition, functioning at a variety of levels. Networking is a survival mechanism and a model of action which goes beyond survival into affirmation, development and growth. Open communication, information and skills sharing and relationship building are all processes which give inner satisfaction as they operate, even if the immediate objective of the action is not always successful. As the networking process is developed – with women as its principal protagonists – so is an optimistic stance towards the real prospect of social transformation. Another word for this is liberation.

REFERENCES

Aird, E. (1985) *From a Different Perspective: Change in Women's Education*. London: Workers' Educational Association.

Armstrong, H. (1986) 'Making the rungs on the ladder: women and community work training'. In Flynn, P. *et al.* (eds) *You're Learning All the Time*. Nottingham: Spokesman.

Bowman, M. (1987) 'Scarlet Productions: a sound vision of equality'. In *The Guardian*, 18 August.

Cox, R. (1988) 'Cruise and Clause 28', in *Women's Studies Newsletter*, **9**. London: Workers' Educational Association.

Flynn, P., Johnson, C., Leiberman, S. and Armstrong, H. (1986) *You're Learning All the Time*. Nottingham: Spokesman.

Keys, D. *et al.* (1983) *Thatcher's Britain: A Guide to the Ruins*. London: Pluto Press in association with *New Socialist*.

Mao Tse-Tung (1968) *Four Essays on Philosophy*. Peking: Foreign Languages Press.

Marshall, M. (1985) *Breaking our Silence: An Introduction*. London: WEA (Workers' Educational Association).

National Institute for Adult Continuing Education (1987) 'Working with women'. In *National REPLAN Bulletin* (Spring).

Neitlich, A. (1985) *Building Bridges: Women's and Men's Liberation*. Cambridge, Massachusetts: [n.p.].

Sheffield Crucible Theatre in Education (1988) *Plague of Innocence*, Teachers' follow-up pack.

Part III

Education, Community and Citizenship

Chapter 11

The Possibilities of Public Life: Educating in the Community

Mark Smith

Current orthodoxy constructs the ideal of citizenship around the values of individualism and the politics of personal responsibility. Mark Smith, drawing on extensive experience of youth and community work and informal education, explores the curricular possibilities of a change of focus from education of the 'Active Citizen' to education for membership of the 'active society'. In seeking a 'more socially just discourse around citizenship', he examines sites outside the system of formal schooling to locate models of practice which help to engage participants with the possibilities of public life. Three main forms of 'educating in the community' are identified and critically evaluated as educative processes: encouraging leadership, enabling partnership, and developing mutual aid. The chapter concludes that education for citizenship in a democratic society must be negotiated through dialogue and experienced as an empowering process.

INTRODUCTION

> The conditions in which we live today and the problems that confront us call for a fresh emphasis in the work of education on the social and civic responsibilities which inevitably await the intelligent citizen.

So wrote Oliver Stanley, then President of the Board of Education, in his foreword to *Education for Citizenship in Secondary Schools* (Association for Education in Citizenship, 1935). More than half a century later, such sentiments would not have been out of place in the deliberations of the Speaker's Commission on Citizenship; in debates regarding cross-curricular themes within the National Curriculum (Fogelman, 1990); or in calls by the Prince of Wales for 100 000 young people a year to devote three months to voluntary work (Johnson, 1989).

The governmental interest in citizenship that emerged in the late 1980s was essentially individualistic and concerned with responsibilities. Discourse was generally constructed in such a way as to overlook questions concerned with rights. For example, the main focus of the Commission on Citizenship was to consider ways of acknowledging voluntary work and decide how to encourage a form of accreditation within schools. There has also been a particular focus on young people and a change in the official language used to describe work with them. For example, whereas the Thompson Report (HMSO, 1982) spoke of social and political education, the HMI report *Effective Youth Work* (DES, 1987) stressed personal and social education. Other government officials emphasized discipline, training and entrepreneurship (Department of Education, 1987). Where *Youth and Community Work in the '70s* (DES, 1969) talked of the 'active society', ministers became more concerned with the 'Active Citizen'. Interest in the unequal nature of power relationships in society, in communal or collective attempts to change or manage things, and in people's rights was not what was required from educators. Instead, the focus was upon enabling individuals to contribute to the economy and to an ordered society, to be compliant workers and good consumers. As citizens they were to respect authority, and give their time to voluntary work and to the care of those in the family. For a privileged number, whose characters were sufficiently formed, there was to be the chance of leadership. For the rest, their role was to be consumers of political decisions rather than the creators of them.

Such an emphasis on service, individual advancement and the capitalist order parallels the redefinition of citizenship in terms of patriotism during the Reagan years in the United States. As Giroux argues in that context, those concerned with social justice need to work to remove the idea of citizenship from forms designed to subordinate citizens to the narrow imperatives of the state. They should work to make citizenship:

> a process of dialogue and commitment rooted in a fundamental belief in the possibility of public life and the development of forms of solidarity that allow people to reflect and organize in order to criticize and constrain the power of the state and to overthrow relations which inhibit and prevent the realization of humanity.
>
> (Giroux, 1989)

In this chapter, we will look at the contribution that educators could make to this task in their work with young people and adults. More specifically, we will be concerned with the activities of educators within autonomous youth groups, enthusiast groups and community organizations. The educational potential of such organizations and the way in which educators may function within them has been an interest of mine for some years (see, for example Smith, 1987a,b) and is currently a central element of an action research project in which I am involved (Smith, 1989). This chapter draws from that work.

EDUCATING IN THE COMMUNITY AND THE POSSIBILITIES OF PUBLIC LIFE

For schools a commitment to a more socially just discourse around citizenship would involve attempting to define them as public spheres where popular engagement and democratic politics can be cultivated (Giroux, 1989). It would mean helping people to 'develop the skills and attitudes of democrats dynamically through the experience of life in a democratic educational institution' (White, 1989). In autonomous community groups many of the structures for 'democratic experience' are already in place. Moreover, the voluntary nature of the contract between learners and educators in such settings and the relative freedom concerning content allow for the possibility of dialogue and commitment. However, what is often lacking is attention to the political and educational tasks involved (Smith, 1987b). Examining the experience of educators within these institutions may help us to think about the sort of changes that are needed within schools.

First, we need to appreciate an important conceptual point. Talking about 'educating in the community' does not mean making a crude distinction between the school or college on one hand and the community on the other. Schools and colleges link into the very social systems that many see as constituting communities (Bell and Newby, 1971). In this sense, educators can be as much 'in the community' when teaching second-year German, as when they are engaged in a heated discussion about local government finance in the tenants' association. Educating in the community is not simply work which takes place beyond the school or college fence. It involves a particular way of making sense of practice and location. In other words, it means looking at the paradigms and processes that practitioners appeal to when thinking about their work. Central to this is reflection on their frame of reference or 'locus of identity' (Wallman, 1984). When approaching the matter in this way, to call someone an educator in the community is to say that his or her professional identity is sustained in significant ways by the structures and forms they associate with a community (Smith, 1988). These structures may be provided by local organizations such as temples and tenants' associations, neighbourly networks and a variety of other everyday situations.

There is an active appreciation of, and engagement with, the social systems through which people operate, and the cultural forms they utilize (Smith, 1988). In many of these structures and processes education will not be a central concern for the people involved. Frequently the role of educators in such situations is to cultivate dialogue; to enable groups or individuals to identify, plan, resource, carry out and assess their own learning projects. The educator's expertise is located in the process of enabling learning rather than in the topic (Jeffs and Smith, 1990).

Several overlapping features of community groups make them sites for convivial practice. First, institutions such as churches, tenants' groups, village hall committees and enthusiast groups usually have an associational structure. That is to say, they have officers, committees and a way of running things which allows members a say and a vote. Within many groups, young people have direct access to this structure: in others they are either ignored or have to fight for recognition. Such local organizations are also part of larger political processes. Initially many were formed to represent people's interests: for example, tenants' action groups and residents' associations. However, they also have to relate to their own regional, national or international bodies. In these ways, local organizations provide the means through which most people engage with the traditional political arena (Entwistle, 1981). By encouraging people to become involved in the running of such groups, we help them to enter organized politics, to engage in public life. That is to say, people are able to join together to learn about and act upon the institutions and processes that significantly affect society or a substantial part of it (Smith, 1987a).

Second, community groups and organizations usually carry within them some valuing of co-operation, a commitment to those in membership, and some understanding of the need for engaging in educational activity. We only have to think about the activities of most religious groups or tenants' groups to confirm this. Much energy is expended in trying to get people to work together and to take their share. The numerous rotas, the discussions about what to do, and the way in which everyday jobs are given a social as well as practical meaning (e.g. gardening or painting parties) are expressions of this.

Further, there is usually an emphasis on giving help to members in trouble or those who need care. We should not fall into the trap of romanticizing the situation: the actual experience of people in such groups may be somewhat different.

Yet the gap between hope and experience is usually recognized in some way. Members may appreciate that there is something more to the group than being organized: that people must be committed to the ideas lying behind the actions and have the capacity to act. For community groups and organizations to remain healthy, attention has to be paid to the education of their members. This may be woven into the fabric of activity through things like the study of sacred writings, listening to sermons, or the reports and briefings at the beginnings of meetings. At other times it may take the form of special events like conferences, study groups or group training.

Third, many community groups may be thought of as mutual aid organizations in themselves. This is because they involve people joining together to produce goods and services for their own enjoyment. The basis is reciprocity and relationships are informed by ideas of 'give and take'. In this they offer an alternative to dominant forms of market and organizational relationships. Bishop and Hoggett (1986) provide numerous examples of this type of group in their study of organizing around enthusiasms. These range from swimming clubs to beekeeping societies and train-spotting circles; from allotment associations to antiques groups and basketball teams. The scope and scale of such groups is huge, yet relatively little attention has been given to them. Further, while the enthusiasm may provide a focus for activity, such groups are far from being wholly concerned with 'doing things'. Much of the reason for their success and endurance is that they fulfil social needs.

This last point directs the way to a fourth and vital consideration. These groups help provide a sense of belonging and identity as well as a setting to meet and make friends with people. Members develop a shared social categorization of themselves in relation to others, a shared perception of 'us' in contrast to 'them' (Turner, 1987). The fact that the group is theirs – or rather ours – and hence owned, quite unlike institutions such as schools, is indicative of the potential and importance of the relationships involved. They play a part in creating social understanding and commitment. The solidarities they foster may well be of a practical, commonsense kind. Sometimes these may be directed towards excluding or subordinating other groupings. Yet these solidarities do still carry within them alternatives to dominating ideologies and practices (Gramsci, 1971). Furthermore, the sense of identity and belonging encouraged (and the practical relationships involved) frequently have a spatial significance. That is to say, many groups are placed 'in the community' or 'in the locality' by their members. At one level this is a rather obvious point, but it can be easily overlooked.

Here we have something of the possibility of public life. Today, that life has largely become a matter of formal obligation.

> Most citizens approach their dealings with the state in a spirit of resigned acquiescence, but this public enervation is in its scope much broader than political affairs. Manners and ritual interchanges with strangers are looked on as at best formal and dry, at worst as phoney. The stranger himself is a threatening figure, and few people can take great pleasure in that world of strangers, the cosmopolitan city.
>
> (Sennett, 1986)

The failure to pay a proper concern to creating and maintaining *res publica* not only makes for the dominance of one group over others, it also deforms private life. 'The world of intimate feelings loses any boundaries, it is no longer restrained by a public world in which people make alternative and countervailing investment of themselves' (Sennett, 1986).

Autonomous community groups and those that 'organize around enthusiasms' provide a powerful possibility, where people are not alienated from the product of their labours, where they can come to an understanding of themselves as active agents, as being able to make a difference, however small. Furthermore, 'such groups can contribute to the process of achieving an active and critical connectedness or nexus both within and beyond ourselves' (Smith, 1988). Their conviviality and potential provide a stark contrast to the deformed relations of production which characterize dominant understandings of the school. However, they are not islands of purity, insulated from evil. Such groups are created and sustained within the 'asymmetrical relations of power that characterize the interplay of dominant and subordinate cultures' (Giroux, 1989). But they are practical responses to the situations that people find themselves in. In this act of creation, this taking of a place in public life, lies hope and possibility.

Beyond participation

It is easy to move from calls for the cultivation of popular engagement and the rejuvenation of public life to earnest discussion regarding the need for more 'participation', implying that somehow the problems of schooling would be solved by the introduction of more participatory ways of working. That path is slippery. Considerable confusion surrounds the word's meaning and use. At one level it simply refers to taking part. However, participation is often used in another, more specific, way. Here, it means being involved in the process of decision making or policy making. Thus, for example, in youth work the Thompson Report argues that participation at club or unit level implies that young people should have a high degree of control over the programme and facilities (HMSO, 1982). This is a common argument, but it is based on a misunderstanding. We need to move beyond the rhetoric.

Being involved in the processes that surround decision making is not the same as the activity of taking decisions. People are often said to have 'participated' when they have been drawn into discussions with policy makers. A group of residents, for example, may be invited to talk with members of a local authority education committee about the needs of their area. What they say may influence the councillors, but the residents are not the people who make the immediate decision. They have no vote in the committee. A lot of the confusion arises from a failure to grasp this simple point. Many different activities are included in the processes which surround decision making, and 'participation' can take place in any one, or all, of them (Richardson, 1983).

The arguments advanced for such 'participation' are varied. First, it is said that such processes are fairer than non-participatory ones. This is because they allow those who will be affected by decisions to have some influence over the outcome. Second, it is often suggested that it aids individual development. It is claimed to help provide those involved with a sense of dignity and self-respect, develop self-confidence, enhance people's knowledge and skills, and to allow people to be more aware of their needs. Third, it is argued that getting people involved in the decision-making process makes for managerial efficiency. Not only are managers provided with more information, but because people feel they have been consulted, they are more likely to agree with the outcome. More than this, it is also sometimes claimed that the exercise of participation shifts power in favour of, for example, the consumers of services.

Each of these blanket assertions is open to question. Where participation is simply considered to be a process of consultation, all that is implied is that others' views are listened to, and not necessarily acted upon. The fairness of many so-called 'participatory' approaches is, therefore, open to question. Similarly, consultation which leads to little or no change is unlikely to enhance self-respect and dignity. Further, much of the learning from taking part in such exercises can be lost if no real effort is made to reflect on what has happened. Here the important factor is less the participation, more the quality of reflection. Lastly, most people who have worked in participative organizations would not want to claim they were efficient. Indeed, they may see efficiency as less important than some other concerns. Listening to people and engaging with their thinking might make a group or organization more effective in certain directions, but not necessarily more efficient (see Stanton, 1989).

Such confusion helps to explain some of the debates about practice. Much of the work labelled participative is often little more than a marketing exercise. We wander round with a clip board asking for suggestions for activities, call meetings to talk about programmes, and so on. Where educators are involved in this process it is often they who make the decisions in the end and do much of the work in putting on activities. This hardly shakes the dominant discourse of schooling, nor alters the relations of production and reproduction.

Leadership, partnership and mutual aid

Moving beyond such changes in style and into the realm of approaches which provide people with an opportunity to take an active part in organizing things does not leave behind confusion and rhetoric. When we examine the practice of those educating in the community three main approaches to this form of working can be seen. These are:

- encouraging leadership
- enabling partnership
- developing mutual aid (based on Smith, 1987a)

We will look at each of these in turn.

Encouraging leadership   This approach can be portrayed as having two main aims. The first is to develop the 'leadership' abilities of those involved. This means improving individuals' decision making and communication, and working on their attitudes or character. A second aim is generally to create an identity with, and understanding of, key institutions and values. For example, in some of the uniformed youth organizations there is a conscious attempt to increase their members' commitment to 'Queen and Country'. However, it is an approach which can also be found in youth clubs, and in community groups and projects.

Leadership approaches generally place an emphasis on organization. They involve creating a hierarchy of jobs and roles. People move through these if workers think they have 'leadership potential'. The obvious examples here are Scouting and Guiding with their structured rules and badges. However, community education workers may similarly use the experience of roles within an organization. For example, tasks like running the bar, taking fees, organizing teams, chairing the users' committee and sitting on the management committee can be employed to develop leadership abilities. We look out for those with potential and encourage them to take up a role. If they do well, people are then promoted to a more important or responsible job. In more 'democratic' organizations workers may even arrange things so that their favoured candidates get elected.

While the focus is on giving people experience of particular roles or tasks there may also be more formal learning activities. Exercises, activities and private study may well be undertaken. A favourite approach with young people is to put them in challenging situations, such as those involved in some, but not all, Outward Bound-type activities, so that they have to take responsibility for themselves and for others. A further important feature of the approach is that a lot of emphasis is put upon the leader or worker as a role model.

There are two immediate problems with these approaches. First, while people do take on more responsibility, they do so in a way which still leaves the educator or organizer at the centre of things. After all, it is they who promote the individuals. Second, having leaders means there must be followers. Encouraging leadership qualities in some individuals can create resignation and acceptance in others. In other words, the approach can be divisive and may actually work against critical thinking. Where government ministers have talked about active citizenship it is usually this model that they are operating within. There is a desire to facilitate the development of a cadre of potential leaders, to nurture structures which allow the building of character. But this character must be of a particular kind: disciplined, responsible, and achievement orientated (Macleod, 1983).

In many instances when we talk of participation, what we in effect mean is developing leadership. As has already been seen, consultative processes can be thought of as entailing participation. When we examine the leadership approach, such consultation as does occur or, indeed, the extent of involvement in direct decision making, is often limited. In particular, the limitations surround *who* is involved. What often happens is that a small group has some say, with the remainder having little.

Enabling partnership If leadership approaches are common within uniformed youth organizations, then partnership is the active approach that is met most often in discussions of 'open' youth work and in many of the initiatives undertaken by community educators based in schools. Again, many of us tend to describe this approach as participatory. For example, a recent report of the National Advisory Council for the Youth Service has this to say (1988):

> Participation in the youth service is sharing responsibility with as many young members or users as possible at all levels. The aim should be to encourage them to initiate and carry through activities and projects and to give them an effective voice in decisions about aims, expenditure and programmes.

What is interesting in this definition, and many like it in youth work and community education, is the emphasis on power sharing. It is the central feature of the approach. Hence, rather than describing the approach as participatory, it is better to view it as enabling partnership. Two aims stand out. The first is to create opportunities for people to take a share with practitioners in the running of the club, group or activity. This involves having a direct role in making decisions and managing activities. The second aim concerns helping people to gain the necessary knowledge, feelings and skills to work with others and to run things. Examples of this approach in action could include:

1. Centre and project meetings between users and workers where decisions are made.
2. The setting up of user groups or *ad hoc* groups in order to organize things and to represent the users to the workers or managers.
3. Training events and workshops to help people gain the relevant skills and knowledge of things like procedures.
4. Work with individuals or with groups on a day-to-day basis as they set about their tasks within the organization.

The tensions in this process are many. For example, there will be clashes between the workers' ideas about a programme and what people want. There is also often a lot of confusion: where educators and users come together in a club or project meeting to talk and makes decisions, who sets the agenda? Who takes the chair? Who has the final say? What usually happens is that the relationship is unequal. There are senior and junior partners. Usually it is the practitioners who are in the driving seat – and at this point partnerships can tip over into a leader–follower relationship.

Effective partnerships are based on agreement. Both sides must freely assent to an action before it can take place. A 'contract' is made between the parties whereby all have a share in the benefits and all take responsibility for any difficulties. For this to happen, considerable effort has to be put into deciding on the terms of the contract, procedures and responsibilities. To do this we have to think about our work in a different way.

Workers who are used to judging the success of a programme by the number or type of events can sometimes find the 'mess' of having to work alongside people really frustrating. Often they are keen to get ahead and get things done. Staying with a group of people who are making mistakes and arguing about who was supposed to have done what can be taxing. Frequently, this feeling arises because we are judging things by the wrong criteria. We focus on the immediate activity or programme rather than what young people are gaining from the process. In other words, it is the learning which is important, rather than the direct outcome of the activity. This is something that school inspectors have also commented upon in the context of youth work:

> Judgments about the quality of youth work essentially are judgments about the quality of the learning experience offered to young people, and not about their relative success or failure in undertaking particular activities.
>
> (DES, 1987)

From this it can be seen that the key concern is less whether a group organizes well, more what they have learnt from the experience.

Developing mutual aid   This third approach places an emphasis upon people organizing things themselves rather than in partnership with workers. The aim is to enable people to gain the knowledge, attitudes and skills necessary to work co-operatively, and to organize in a way which brings collective benefit and enjoyment. The enthusiast clubs analysed by Bishop and Hoggett (1986) provide an obvious example of this approach. While many of these groups are initiated from within their potential membership, community educators also have a very significant role – particularly in those activities where there has not been a strong tradition of organizing in a particular community. Some of the most spectacular work in this respect (in terms of scale) has been associated with the development of participation in sports and in initiatives such as Actionsport. Within the community development arena, the establishing and main-taining of such groups, whether they be community associations, savings clubs or playgroups, has been a predominant concern of workers. Such interests also have a long history in youth work. It is often forgotten that, for example, the Albemarle Report on the Youth Service laid particular stress upon this approach (HMSO, 1960):

> We value very highly the active participation of the young and their own leadership of groups which they bring into existence themselves . . . This means in practice that we . . . should accept, as a proper part of the Service, spontaneous but ephemeral units which may spring up and passionately absorb the energies of their members for two or three years and then fade away as the members grow out of them.

The report described this approach as self-determination. Here I have preferred to emphasize the social and mutual nature of the relationships in such groups. Thus within this approach workers are likely to:

1. Work with groups of people who either want to organize campaigns or provision for themselves or are already doing so.
2. Run workshops and training events to help people gain particular skills.
3. Provide certain material resources such as access to office equipment or a room to meet.

Working in this way demands that community educators think of themselves as facilitators rather than organizers. It also involves making clear the boundaries between the duties of educators and those they work with. One of the sternest tests of this approach is in work with young people, where there is often an almost automatic assumption of responsibility by the 'adult' workers. For example, let us consider what happens when we have responsibility for the building in which a group of young people meet. In the mutual aid approach, those young people would have to hire the building or room from us. They would then organize the use they made of the facility and take responsibility for what happens during their sessions. This situation is akin to what happens in community associations. There groups have to abide by certain rules when they use a room or hall. Provided those rules are adhered to, and the objects of the group are in keeping with the values of the association, then the officers or workers will have little to say about the day-to-day running of the group – unless, that is, the group wants help.

We can see in community associations a pattern of organization which could be used by others. For example, local religious groups could look to such structures to cast light on their relationship with groups of young people wanting to run something themselves. Within associations there are usually directly organized 'sections' and groups who affiliate. There might be an old-time dancing section: to join it you become a member of the association and the dancing is an association activity. Both forms contribute to the whole and have to abide by the rules of the association. Similarly, both are likely to take part in the management and running of the association and in its wider work, perhaps, say, to improve local services. However, while sections are, in the end, managed by the association, affiliates run themselves. Rather than thinking of educational provision in terms of directly organized activities (or 'sections'), perhaps we need to focus more strongly on the idea of affiliated groups.

Community associations have also provided some workers with a model for the way in which young people's organizations and other community education initiatives can develop (see, for example, Richards, 1987; Cann, 1989). We can see why when we look at the purposes of a community association. These may be summarized as follows (National Federation of Community Associations, 1974):

1.   To bring individuals together.
2.   To bring together the other organizations in the locality.
3.   To provide opportunities for leisure-time activities in response to local needs.
4.   To provide a basis for an education in democratic practice.
5.   To see that gaps in community service are filled.
6.   To manage the community centre.
7.   To provide a corporate voice for the local community.

What, in effect, some workers have done is to encourage the formation of a youth or community education association, rather than a community association. This body then undertakes the above tasks. Often there is also an emphasis upon developing self-programming groups who affiliate to the association. It is then they who provide the bulk of the activities.

The advantage of a mutual aid approach is that it can provide people with a sense of ownership unlike that found in partnership. People are literally doing things for themselves. Nevertheless, it is not without problems. Sometimes the tasks involved can appear to be complicated and onerous – so much so that many people may be put off doing things. Here we may be tempted to fall back on the idea of partnership. However, the alternative is to work with people to break down the tasks into smaller components that are manageable: also we may encourage groups to be more modest in their initial aims. We might contract to deliver services to a group: these might include such facilities as a coffee bar or the provision of instructors. But care has to be taken when doing this that practitioners do not drop back into the role of provider. They have to remind themselves that the difference between this approach and partnership is that the group remains responsible, i.e. they are simply buying-in services, rather than running them jointly.

A further concern is that groups become dependent on the energy and expertise of a small number of people. It could be argued that what happens in youth work is that you simply replace the practitioners with more youthful organizers. However, there is a crucial difference in the way that group members view those who organize. As Bishop and Hoggett (1986) put it: in one case the organizing is done 'by some of us for all of us'; in the other it is performed 'by them for us'.

There will always be some tension with regard to this. Some will feel they are 'doing it all' or that 'people just sit on their backsides', while others will resent this person or that person always taking the limelight. One of the things that practitioners need to do is to enable those involved to reflect upon such difficulties. In other words, they will have to stress that mutual aid involves cooperation, reciprocity and working for collective benefit and enjoyment.

Lastly, there is the perennial problem associated with special-interest groups – that they become absorbed in their own activities. This concern is often heard in community associations in respect of sections and affiliated groups. People are thought only to be interested in their own corner rather than the whole. Care has be taken not to strengthen narrow ideas of self-interest. We have to work to develop people's appreciation of, and commitment to, wider ideas of public life.

Towards mutual aid

When we put these three approaches side-by-side a number of important things become clear (see Figure 11.1). First, as we move from left to right, there is a shift in practitioners' responsibilities. In the leadership approach they have overall control; in partnership it is shared; and in the mutual aid approach they have no hand in the direct management of the group. Second, there is a movement away from an emphasis upon individual achievement (and often competition). Instead there is a valuing of collective and co-operative efforts within those community groups that adopt this way of thinking and acting. This does not mean that there is not a concern with the group or the team in the leadership approach, nor an interest in the individual in the mutual aid approach. Rather, it implies that there is a difference in focus. Third, the mutual aid approach places an emphasis upon smaller, self-determining groups. As a result, it can mean that members have a greater opportunity to be directly involved in running the groups. This is part of movement from an organization- to a person-centred orientation.

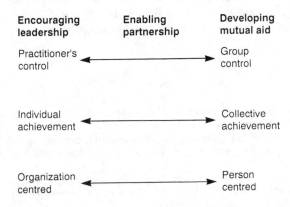

Figure 11.1 Approaches to working with people who want to take an active part in organizing.

It would seem that the mutual aid approach provides community educators and participants with considerable scope. Two things are especially worth noting here. First, it is important to recognize people's feelings and experiences. Many people want to do more than consume ready-made leisure packages. Rather, they want to make something for themselves. This is partly connected to a wish to be, and to act, with other people. For young people, there is also the wish to be seen as adult. Taking responsibility for something yourself is seen to be more adult than someone taking it for you, or even sharing it with you.

Second, the concern with mutual aid has to be put into the wider political context. If we wish to have a society in which there is a vibrant public life characterized by dialogue, mutuality and commitment, we need institutions which aid such processes. We also need places where we can learn to think and act politically. As Freire (1974) has said of Brazil:

> People could learn social and political responsibility only by experiencing that responsibility, through intervention in the destiny of their children's schools, in the destinies of their trade unions and places of employment through associations, clubs and councils, and in the life of their neighbourhoods, churches and rural communities by actively participating in associations, clubs and charitable societies.

It is through these smaller-scale bodies that most of us engage with politics. For a democratic discourse to flourish it is critical to have 'citizens' groups which participate vigorously in the political process' (Twelvetrees, 1985). What is being suggested is that we must work to reconstruct our understanding of schools to take account of this. We need to move beyond a view of them as somehow being separate from the communities in which they are located. This is not some simplistic call for teachers to make alliances with groups and movements 'outside' schools: rather it is to interrogate our whole way of thinking. Our practice needs to be more firmly grounded in the lived experiences of those we work with. We need to nurture within schools such autonomous organizational forms as we have been discussing here – however fraught with difficulties this might be (Smith, 1987a; Tapper and Salter, 1978). The discourse of schooling needs radical attention if we are truly to cultivate dialogical communities in which justice, wisdom and connectedness are concretely embodied in everyday practices. It is not only that schools need to be defined as 'public spheres where the dynamics of popular engagement and democratic politics can be cultivated' (Giroux, 1989); our daily practice as educators must also be reframed in terms of the dialogical possibilities of public life.

REFERENCES

Association for Education in Citizenship (1935) *Education for Citizenship in Secondary Schools*. London: Oxford University Press.

Bell, C. and Newby, H. (1971) *Community Studies*. London: George Allen & Unwin.

Bishop, J. and Hoggett, P. (1986) *Organizing around Enthusiasms: Mutual Aid in Leisure*. London: Comedia.

Cann, R. (1989) 'Portuguese popular associations'. *Adult Learning*, 1 (2), 52–3.

Department of Education and Science (1969) *Youth and Community Work in the '70s* (The Fairbairn–Milson Report). London: HMSO.

Department of Education and Science (1987) *Education Observed 6: Effective Youth Work. A Report by HM Inspectors*. London: DES.

Department of Education for Northern Ireland (1987) *Policy for the Youth Service in Northern Ireland*. Belfast: Department of Education.

Entwistle, H. (1981) 'The political education of adults'. In D. Heater and J.A. Gillespie (eds) *Political Education in Flux*. London: Sage.

Fogelman, K. (1990) 'Citizenship in secondary schools: a national survey (Summary report)'. Mimeographed paper.

Freire, P. (1974) *Education: The Practice of Freedom*. London: Writers and Readers.

Giroux, H.A. (1989) *Schooling for Democracy: Critical Pedagogy in the Modern Age*. London: Routledge.

Gramsci, A. (1971) *Selections from Prison Notebooks*. London: Lawrence & Wishart.

Heller, A. (1976) 'Marx's theory of revolution and the revolution in everyday life'. In A. Heller *et al.* (eds) *The Humanization of Socialism*. London: Allison & Busby.

HMSO (1960) *The Youth Service in England and Wales* (The Albemarle Report). London: HMSO.

HMSO (1982) *Experience and Participation* (The Thompson Report). London: HMSO.

Jeffs, T. and Smith, M. (1990) 'Using informal education'. In T. Jeffs and M. Smith (eds) *Using Informal Education: An Alternative to Casework, Teaching and Control?* Buckingham: Open University Press.

Johnson, A. (1989) 'Prince backs army of youth to care for old'. *The Guardian*, 4 September.

Macleod, D. I. (1983) *Building Character in the American Boy: The Boy Scouts, YMCA and their Forerunners, 1870–1920*. Madison, Wisconsin: University of Wisconsin Press.

National Advisory Council for the Youth Service (1988) *Participation Part A: Guidelines for Youth Service Policy Makers*. London: DES.

National Federation of Community Associations (1974) *Creative Living. The Work and Purposes of a Community Association*. London: National Council of Social Service.

Richards, K. (1987) 'Neighbourhood centres, not community schools'. In G. Allen, J. Bastiani, I. Martin and K. Richards (eds) *Community Education: An Agenda for Educational Reform*. Milton Keynes: Open University Press.

Richardson, A. (1983) *Participation*. London: Routledge & Kegan Paul.

Sennett, R. (1986) *The Fall of Public Man*. London: Faber.

Smith, M. (1987a) Political education: approaches in the community. Newcastle: Youth and Policy. Occasional paper 4.

Smith, M. (1987b) 'Non-formal political education with young people'. In C. Harber (ed.) *Political Education in Britain*. Lewes: Falmer Press.

Smith, M. (1988) *Developing Youth Work: Informal education, Mutual Aid and Popular Practice*. Milton Keynes: Open University Press.

Smith, M. (ed.) (1989) '*Youth or Adult?' Working Papers 1*. London: YMCA National College/The Rank Foundation.

Stanton, A. (1989) *Invitation to Self-Management*. Ruislip: Dab Hand Press.

Tapper, T. and Salter, B. (1978) *Education and the Political Order: Changing Patterns of Class Control*. London: Macmillan.

Turner, J. C. (1987) *Rediscovering the Social Group: A Self-Categorization Theory*. Oxford: Basil Blackwell.

Twelvetrees, A. (1985) *Democracy and the Neighbourhood*. London: National Federation of Community Organisations.

Wallman, S. (1984) *Eight London Households*. London: Tavistock.

White, P. (1989) 'Educating courageous citizens'. In C. Harber and R. Meighan (eds) *The Democratic School*. Ticknall, Derby: Education Now Books.

Chapter 12

Education for Community in the 1990s: A Christian Perspective

David Clark

David Clark argues that the Christian concept of 'kingdom' shows how education for community can help to counter what he perceives to be the pervasive threat of 'psychological fragmentation and social disintegration'. Education has a crucial role to play in constructing a coherent yet open definition of community in a rapidly changing and increasingly pluralistic society. On the other hand, community – understood as a quality of social relations which confers security, significance and solidarity upon all its members – is itself a necessary precondition for effective and responsive education. The implications of recent educational reform for the communalization of education are examined in the light of the dual claim that there can be 'no community without education' and 'no education without community'. The potentially positive effects of recent legislation can only be realized if educators, operating as catalysts on the boundaries between cultures, can transform their theory and practice within a new and visionary praxis.

INTRODUCTION

If you always do what you do, you'll only get what you've got

(Graffiti, Washington, DC, 1985)

So begins the final chapter of Handy and Aitken's (1986) seminal book about schools as organizations. The sentence is a pithy critique of an approach to the 1990s which cannot hope to meet the challenges of the decade ahead, in educational or any other terms. For we are now entering a time of such unprecedented change that even those of the twentieth century as a whole are likely to pale into insignificance.

The prophets of the new age to come have been numerous. From Roszak to Toffler, from Berger to Capra, the signs of things to come have been pointed up for us to reflect upon. But now many of these signs are already realities and beginning to awaken not only our imagination but to impinge directly on the everyday routines of our lives.

One dominant theme that permeates the writings of all the prophets of our age is that of pluralism. Human differences and diversity have always existed. But now we can know what a cultural kaleidoscope our world really is simply by driving through any major city. High-rise office blocks dwarf the once admired Victorian town hall, the banking district sports the names of every continent under the sun, Asian and English stalls compete for space in the marketplace, the plushy renovated apartment blocks for the young and upwardly mobile squeeze in among crumbling old tenements inhabited by the new underclasses, and the glittering mosque stands defiantly alongside the begrimed parish church.

THE SEARCH FOR COMMUNITY

These things have come to stay. The technological revolution of recent decades has ensured that our world is destined to become even smaller. Distance has been almost obliterated; time is now the main measure of apartness, and that is being ever reduced in length by the mind-blowing acceleration in communications and human mobility.

For all its welter of innovation and change, however, our world still faces the age-old question with which every generation has struggled: 'Wherein can community be found?' Or, to put it in more biblical terms: 'Who is my neighbour?' As the diversity of the human race thrusts itself ever more bewilderingly upon us, bringing, as Peter Berger (1980) put it, 'the vertigo of relativity' to our life-styles, values and beliefs, how can we retain a personal and social equilibrium which can prevent psychological fragmentation and social disintegration? Parker Palmer was certainly right when he wrote: 'Community means more than the comfort of souls. It means, and has always meant, the survival of the species' (1977).

This search for community has two facets of vital importance to educationalists. One is the clear need for human beings to have their roots sunk deep enough in a familiar cultural soil to enable them to withstand the powerful winds of change now blowing across the globe. The danger here is that the home can become a prison, the local patch a ghetto. The other is the need for all groups and all 'tribes' to open themselves to new experiences and wider horizons, to the creation of new cultures. The problem here is that the brave new world can become rootless and threaten all with anomie and self-destruction. What we seek, therefore, is 'a third way', beyond the claustrophobia of the local and the impersonality of the cosmopolitan.

NO COMMUNITY WITHOUT EDUCATION

By whatever means such a 'third way' is to emerge – and emerge it must if 'the species' is 'to survive' – education will have a key part to play. The first of two fundamental points that this chapter wishes to argue is, therefore, that *there can be no community without education*.

This statement would seem innocuous, even trite, were it not for the fact that 'education' has itself been seduced by the attractions of the technological revolution, though some would argue that the rot set in with the Enlightenment's whole-hearted espousal of the age of reason (for example, see Newbigin, 1986). In brief, 'educationalists' have been ever more prone to shift from the openness of genuine education to a subtle and often unrecognized form of indoctrination. Such a prostituting of education's most important task, that of opening up mind and heart to the multifaceted and mysterious nature of our universe, to the complexity and the wonder of being human and, above all, to questions of meaning and purpose as well as function and usefulness, blocks the search for that quality and those forms of community which must be found if the human race is to survive the twenty-first century. Without education no 'third way' can be discovered.

What are the substitutes which we so easily mistake for the real thing? Figure 12.1 summarizes a response to this question which would otherwise be over-lengthy.

	INDOCTRINATION	NURTURE	INSTRUCTION	TRAINING	EDUCATION
		Educare (to mould or train)			*Educere* (to lead out)
AIM	Conditioning	Socialization	Imparting knowledge	Imparting skills	Animating and empowering
FOCUS	'The cause' or 'The system'	Culture	Subject	Technique	Life and the person
RATIONALITY	Irrational (ignores evidence)	Non-rational (accepts evidence)			Rational (questions evidence)
METHOD	Imprinting	Assimilation	Memorizing — Understanding — Mastery		Discovery and commitment
CHOICE	Determined by the 'teacher'	Determined by the tradition	Determined by the curriculum		Open – towards a new culture
TYPE OF AUTHORITY	Autocratic – imposes	Paternal/ maternal – guards and guides	Directive Informs and explains	Demonstrates and practises	Democratic – shares and enables
MORALITY	Immoral (ignores or distorts values)	Non-moral (accepts values)			Moral (questions in order to develop values)

——————— TOWARDS EDUCATION ———————→

Figure 12.1 Approaches to learning.

The teacher's dilemma is that, while nurture, instruction and training are all essential ingredients of education, they are only a preparation for, not identical with, the genuine article. Even more dangerous is the fact that if the learning process is taken as synonymous with only nurture, instruction or training, then we are likely to end up with indoctrination of some kind or other.

If the evident and ever more intrusive plurality of our world means that fresh ways of living together must be found; if we are, like it or not, having to embark on a search for new forms of community which can satisfy and sustain us as adequately as the tribe did in the past, but which can now embrace many other tribes as well; if we have to seek and find a 'new culture' which can hold together existing cultures, ancient and modern, in a communally viable and enriching whole; then only genuine education, as the open-ended search for new knowledge, understanding, insight and experience, will suffice. There can be no community without education.

Christian perspectives on education

The Christian's journey of faith has a great deal in common with the communal quest outlined above. For some, it simply throws new light on that task; for others, myself included, it offers the perspective and the dynamism without which that quest is impossible. But whatever one's standpoint, the Christian contribution to the search for new forms of human togetherness has much to teach us.

The Christian faith has most to offer those engaged in the communal quest when the concept of 'the kingdom' is brought to the fore. It would be helpful if a term other than 'kingdom' could be found as today this can appear overly male and imperialistic. But it is difficult to find a more accurate word to translate the Greek *basileia*. The best that can be done, therefore, is to remember that in the New Testament Christ's use of 'kingdom' has its own very special meaning.

Christ described the kingdom as a treasure so precious that a man would sell all he had in order to buy the field where he found it buried, or cash in all his pearls so that he could purchase the pearl of greatest value. So it is today, I believe, with community. At its fullest and richest, it is that which is worth all our industrial, scientific and technological revolutions put together. Seek first the kingdom, Christ declared, and all else will follow; seek community first and all else falls into place.

It is important to note that Christ talks about the kingdom having to be discovered. It is there but it is 'hidden', in part because the kingdom is experienced through very ordinary things like mustard seed, or leaven in bread; but also, in part, because its delivery is not so much 'out there' as within us. We find it when we can say: 'I was blind; now I see.'

In all this Christ was describing the nature of the kingdom. But he was also setting out a masterful apologetic for the nature of true learning. For community, like the kingdom, is likewise often 'hidden'; its meaning and its nature have to be discovered. This is not just because community can be overlooked through its very ordinariness – for it is present in every caring home, every healthy association and every humane society – but because we can only own it if we have discovered it for ourselves. No years of socialization, no programme of instruction or training, can substitute for that educational process through which we ourselves encounter new experiences and discover new dimensions of what community can mean.

The search for the kingdom also reminds us that the true learning process is a journey, often tough and dangerous, because, in cultural terms, we have to break clear from the restrictiveness of the past if we are to embrace a new and more open vision of the future. To break out of our cultural home, leave our native land, without devaluing what they have offered us, is an essential aspect of the journey towards new communal forms. But such a breakthrough (or break-out) can only occur where men and women have come to appreciate what genuine education is all about.

Christ not only preached the kingdom, he taught people how to go about finding it.

He was the great educator! He encouraged people to move on and opened up new vistas, not by dogmatic pronouncement or long didactic discourse, but by telling stories and asking questions. Who else could have been less like the traditional instructor or trainer? Who could have played the role of resource person and enabler better? If the professional teacher is to lead people to grasp something of the new vision of community, Christ is a model we ignore at our peril.

What of the Education Reform Act?

If there can be no community without education, has the 1988 Education Reform Act (ERA) moved us on or taken us backward in this all-important quest? In brief, how genuinely educational is the legislation which has now been enacted? In the communal context this is the central question. The honest answer is that we do not yet know. It all depends on how the Act works out in practice at national and local level. We are only just at the outset of a decade of manoeuvring, of adjustments and readjustments, as well as of just plain confrontation. But some pointers exist.

Educationally, some of the most significant clauses of the Act relate not so much to pupils or school staff, but to 'adults other than teachers'. It is (in particular) parents who are singled out for the widening of horizons and the expansion of choice. Open enrolment, parental influence on governing bodies, parental access to information, not least their offspring's test scores, as well as a parental voice in deciding whether a school should or should not opt out, all appear, at least at first sight, educationally sound. In some ways, these clauses in the Act have called the bluff of some community educators who are now beating a hasty retreat into a call for more professional control. But, in the light of our argument that the creation of new communal forms depends on people exercising their own informed judgements, the Act's insistence on greater parental involvement and choice is to be welcomed.

So too, on similar grounds, must local financial management receive at least two cheers. To be master or a mistress of one's own route planning and route finding is educationally a good starting point. The search for community cannot be a creative one if schools are kept in a state of immature dependence on local authorities or any other kind of 'big brother'. If parents have educationally benefited from certain aspects of ERA, then headteachers and governors are also potential beneficiaries.

But, and it is a big 'but', there are at least three major problems with which the Act has left us. It is as yet quite unclear as to how much control the Secretary of State will exercise over all the possible choices he has offered parents, headteachers and governors. With massive powers now located in his person he could easily destroy the genuinely educational potential of these parts of the Act in pursuit of a narrow political dogma.

A second problem is the degree to which the principles of educational and communal openness offered to parents, heads and governors, will be used to widen choice and extend horizons, or to protect their own 'tribe' and restrict opportunity to 'the chosen people'.

Thirdly, extending an educational approach to parents and other adults seems to have, by and large, by-passed pupils and teachers. The National Curriculum is a highly ambiguous learning tool. It could help to give pupils that so-called 'entitlement' so long overdue. It could also become a very 'uneducational' instrument of the state verging on indoctrination. Overall, the National Curriculum would seem to have more in common with instruction and training than with the kind of education needed for the communal regeneration of our society. Wider perspectives are discernible, for example in certain of the cross-curricular dimensions such as personal and social development, or themes such as citizenship, but as yet they are few and far between. There is no guarantee whatsoever that the cultural context fostered by the Act will be as open and rich as the communal needs of the 1990s demand.

The role of the teacher

If the discovery of new ways of living together as human beings is now the most critical challenge facing our world, then not only education but educationalists have a supremely important part to play. It is unclear whether ERA will enhance or limit this key role.

Two developments are necessary. First, the search for community ahead of us will require that *all* become teachers, as well as learners. The task is just too big for the small band of professionals available. The other is that professional teachers will, in future, need to fulfil a very different role. From being the ground of all knowledge, teachers will have to move to becoming well-informed guides to the extensive founts of knowledge that now exist in a thousand and one places within and beyond the school or other educational agency. This will mean a quite different training, the emphasis on the skills of the resource person rather than those of the instructor. It will also require a more mobile function, with the classroom regarded as a base-camp rather than the all-purpose learning enclosure it is at present. It is the kind of role which, in many ways, Christ 'the great educator' foreshadowed twenty centuries ago.

Even more important in the context of the search for community, the teacher will need to work on the boundary *between* cultures, with the vital task of enabling their members to cross and surmount cultural divides in search of the new communal forms now urgently needed. In his dealings with rich and poor, male and female, Jew and Gentile, Christ presented an impressive model of what is wanted. It is a task which requires of 'the teacher' the ability to raise questions and challenge obstructive dogmatisms in a way which opens up new horizons without undue threat or anxiety. It is a highly skilled task, requiring abilities ranging from multicultural awareness to group work and effective management, for which those only concerned with nurture, instruction or training are often quite unprepared. The Education Reform Act, preoccupied as it seems to be with a highly structured and content-oriented approach to curriculum development, offers little help here. With able educational facilitators, the quest for community will be a formidable undertaking, to say the least. Without them, it will be virtually a non-starter.

'The communal dilemma'

All this raises the sixty-four thousand dollar question as to how genuinely educational the Education Reform Act really is. What will happen if those given choice do not choose what the government wants?

Here we come face to face with 'the communal dilemma': that situation where the hope of widening communal horizons encounters a powerful determination to retain a particular cultural or, in this case, political identity. By and large, governments are more concerned with the latter than the former; educationalists with the former rather than the latter.

The temptation for any government is to redefine 'education' in its own terms; to seek to make its political message (such as 'efficiency' or 'enterprise') the medium. But in the face of the changes and challenges outlined at the beginning of this chapter, such an approach to learning cannot suffice. For our society and our world to survive, the quest for community is a matter of the utmost urgency and must, in the name of cultural or political identity, be pursued with as little restriction as possible. There can be no community without education. But also *there can be no education without community*.

NO EDUCATION WITHOUT COMMUNITY

If the quest for new forms of community depends on genuine education to open up new cultural possibilities, then it is also true that such learning can only occur where the communal context is favourable. It is in one sense a chicken and egg situation. Either the developing chicken or the hatching egg can move us on. This process is illustrated in Figure 12.2.

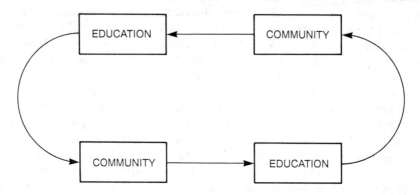

Figure 12.2

So far we have explored 'education' as the catalyst for beginning the journey towards a wider culture. In what follows, it is 'community' which becomes the key concept. It moves from being the 'end' to being the 'means'. The journey in search of a new understanding of what it means to be 'one world' can only be achieved if the company within which we pursue it is as genuinely communal as the educational process is genuinely educational. So what does 'genuinely communal' mean?

The essentials of community

Here we have to distinguish between 'culture' and 'community'. The 'cultural wheel' (see Figure 12.3) consists of the plurality of economic, social and religious forms, through which community is expressed. These forms embrace the territory people occupy, the relationships they develop, the interactions between them and the values they hold dear. Yet, despite this diversity, the 'communal spokes' binding all cultures together are limited in number. I have summarized the former, as 'the three S's' (Clark, 1989): a sense of security, a sense of significance and a sense of solidarity.

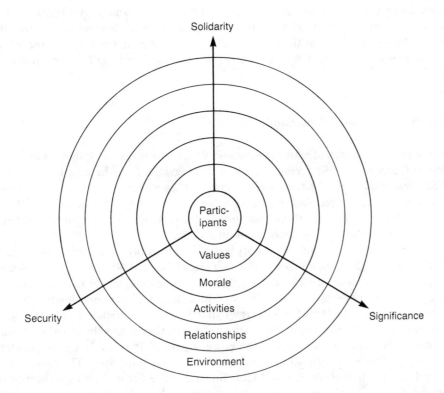

Figure 12.3 The 'cultural wheel' and 'communal spokes'.

The *sense of security* is the most earthy of the communal components. It is that sentiment which enables people to feel they are safe from the threat of physical harm or social violence. It is about feeling 'at home' in a strange and dangerous world, perhaps more obvious among those living close to nature, but still very real today for all of us. The task of the educator here is to sustain a nurturing environment for the learner.

Significance is about a sense of identity and dignity, personally as well as culturally. It exists where people feel they are valued by others, have a role to play and a destiny to fulfil. The task of the educator is here that of affirming people for who they are as well as what they are.

Solidarity is concerned with a sense of belonging, of togetherness, of being one with others. It is that sentiment which points in the direction of collaboration and partner-ship. The task of the educator is to further friendships and alliances, a sense of the 'we' over against merely the 'I'.

Genuine community, like genuine education, means the opening up of these commu-nal dimensions as fully as possible, without creating undue threat or anxiety for those involved. The task of the community educator is not simply to strengthen but to broaden these communal experiences. Genuine community making is about finding a *more* secure place to stand, a *more* fulfilling role to play and a *wider* world to which to belong.

The three communal components are intimately related; none can survive or develop without the others being present. Yet they have a kind of Maslovian relationship, security being the most basic and solidarity the most 'advanced'. If, using different terminology, we can speak of security as the experience of dependence on the other things and persons we all at times need, of significance as independence, and of soli-darity as interdependence, then it is the last that describes the quest for community in its fullest sense.

Christian perspectives on community

Again, it is the Christian idea of the kingdom which throws as much light as any on the concept of community. Speaking strictly in theological terms, the kingdom means the rule or reign of God. But I have argued elsewhere (Clark, 1987), from a more sociologi-cal perspective, that there can be no rule without a community among whom it is exercised. Thus, I like to think not only of the kingdom, but of the kingdom *community*, with the last word giving colour and depth.

The nature of the kingdom community is depicted not only by the words and deeds of Christ but by the Christian image of the Trinity (see Clark, 1989) which, as both doctrine and symbol, offers some important insights into the meaning of our key concept.

The Trinity is made up of three Persons in a deep and personal relationship: the Father, the Son and the Holy Spirit. It is a dynamic relationship based on the life-giving and loving interactions of equal yet unique partners. This is how the kingdom commu-nity 'on earth as in heaven' must, therefore, operate. It is made up of persons in life-giving and loving relationships, both intimate and empowering. The symbol of the Trinity describes the Father, Son and Holy Spirit as quite distinct, yet as a wholly united Godhead. So, too, the kingdom community, here and hereafter, recognizes its members as unique persons, yet drawn ever closer together by the mutual exchange of life and love. The Trinity, with the kingdom community, is, I believe, the most profound repre-sentation of divine and human interdependence we can find.

The three Persons of the Trinity offer a new perspective on the meaning of our three S's. God as 'the Creator' can be said to symbolize the source of security and well-being within the kingdom community. God is here both Father and Mother. Christ, as 'the Liberator', meets our human yearning for freedom and autonomy, both individually and collectively. The Holy Spirit, 'the Unifier', points those in search of the kingdom community to the hope of a universal solidarity.

Yet there is a flip-side to these divine representations of our three S's. And here we must also turn to Christ's deeds and words as recorded in the Gospels. God as Creator is shown there as caring, above all, for what is vulnerable within creation, be that the grass of the field, sparrows at ten-a-penny or the sick and disabled in body and mind. Thus, within the kingdom community it is the most vulnerable who are our first concern. Christ as Liberator spends his life's work seeking to free people from the captivity of self and systems in their many different guises. He shows that within the kingdom community the priority must go to those enslaved by their own or others' wilfulness and evil intent. The Holy Spirit as Unifier is about the business of reconciliation and justice. So, to grow, the kingdom community must manifest the process of reconciliation and the quest for justice and peace as of paramount importance.

All these emphases indicate that the kingdom community reverses human priorities. The kingdom community is about what Christians today are calling 'the option for the poor'. It is about society being judged first and foremost by the condition of the weakest, not the strongest or most 'successful', of its members. It is about power sharing and corporate accountability.

The role that Christ played in proclaiming the kingdom was that of 'vision manager'. Not only was he a teacher *par excellence*, but one who also knew that 'without a vision the people perish'. The vision to which he pointed men and women was of a kingdom to come, the final triumphant vindication of his own ministry and the open acknowledgement by all people of the sovereignty of God. Though Christ set up no great organization to promote his views and values, it was this vision that gave his followers the courage to carry the Gospel to the ends of the earth.

Christ's vision was not Utopian. The kingdom was to come, but it was also *already* here. It could be personally experienced in the life and deeds also of Christ himself. It was a kingdom earthed – incarnated – in real people and real living. It was about conflict as well as reconciliation, pain as well as joy. Its signs were there to point people to a new and amazing future, but they were signs grounded in the everyday experiences of being human. Christ's genius, the divine genius, was that the hope he brought was not 'pie in the sky when you die', but a vision that connected earth and heaven without denying the realities of either.

THE EDUCATION REFORM ACT

The earthed vision of the kingdom community is one reason why it is in no way absurd to turn from the Gospels to government legislation. For, in one sense, the Education Reform Act is also an attempt to be both practical and visionary. In communal terms, does it succeed?

ERA is obviously concerned about the first S – security – though this is not spelled out in any explicit way in the legislation. But, political ideology apart, it is clear that the government is concerned at Britain's economic stagnation and its inability to ensure an economically secure future for our children. The recovery of a sound material base to life and living is clearly a major concern as an underlying *raison d'être* of the Act. There is, however, little overt recognition that 'security' may be related to much more than ever-increasing economic wealth and that the means by which this is achieved could be more important than the end.

The means by which the government seeks to promote national regeneration is that of individual endeavour and initiative. It is personal enterprise which is to bring social salvation. In this, the Act homes in strongly on our second S – significance. The impetus for many of the 'reforms', including the National Curriculum, is the assumption that most pupils want to gain significance, not least in terms of publicly defined and acclaimed attainment targets.

The problem here is that the use of the desire for significance as the driving force of communal renewal devalues the third and even more important S – solidarity. The job of the pupil is to jump through the hoops of personal achievement, with many attainment tasks being powerfully influenced by the instrumentality of a technological age; the ability to work as a team or in partnership with others is incidental. Assessment and testing are targeted at the individual. The 'success' of schools is to be judged by the summation of how well individual pupils have attained the set tasks. The disappointment here is not that individual endeavour looms large – a weakness which the old examination system also perpetrated – but that a golden opportunity to move towards more corporate communal goals has been lost.

The problem is not simply that pupil is separated off from pupil. It is a failure to recognize that the third S – solidarity – has to be an essential ingredient within our ever more pluralistic society if we are to emerge from the economic as well as social problems which beset us. To overstress the individual ('there is no such thing as society'), to neglect the need to work towards a more genuinely multicultural community, is to underestimate the crucial foundation on which our future well-being, social *and* material, has to be built. Active recognition of our interdependence is a *sine qua non* of survival, in all ways, in the world of the twenty-first century.

Potentially as serious is ERA's over-emphasis on the separateness of each school. To stress local autonomy is educationally sound, as already noted. But to seek to increase 'effectiveness' by the thinly veiled promotion of aggressive competition is a very dangerous course to pursue. If open enrolment and local management turn schools into mini-industrial enterprises, vying for 'bottoms on chairs' at £X a time, then the search for that communal experience able to carry us through the years ahead is doomed. What is more, education itself will be sold short, for there can be no true education without community. The context of learning will circumscribe its essential openness to the whole world beyond, the medium will deny the message. And to seek to do no more than genuflect to community by squeezing an ambiguous theme called 'citizenship' in by the back door will do nothing to match the countervailing forces.

The potentially destructive ideology of competition inherent in the Act does even less to meet the needs of the vulnerable and marginalized. If the Christian concept of the kingdom community is taken seriously, then the success of a nation is judged by its concern for its weakest and poorest members. An education system built on a competitiveness which outweighs collaboration cannot hope to offer justice to the disadvantaged. Both pupils and schools set in situations of deprivation can hope for little from an Act which encourages each educational unit to gain and keep whatever it can exclusively for its own use.

The consequence of this is not simply that the rich will grow richer and the poor poorer, but that we shall *all* – in educational terms at least – lose out. For schools which by choice or force have their experiences of community circumscribed will have a stunted experience of education. The suburb that knows nothing of the ghetto is as deprived as the ghetto which is prevented from learning anything about the suburb.

The 'Great Debate' of the future will be as much about community as education. It will be about how to raise the quality of the medium as much as the message. It will be about how schools, and all other agencies for learning, can enter into an increasing sense of partnership, of their solidarity with every sector of society, from home to hospital, from farm to factory, in the pursuit of both excellence *and* equality. For the school which denies or devalues what other schools, other neighbourhoods and other sectors of society can offer it, through vigorous collaboration and not just occasional exchanges, will, in the context of the pluralistic world into which we are rapidly moving, be educationally the greatest failure.

In this 'Great Debate' we need many 'vision managers', for 'without a vision the people will perish'. As Christ inspired his followers by his vision of the kingdom as well as by his deeds, so we now need headteachers and others with major responsibility who can offer us a life-giving and compassionate hope for the years ahead. As with the vision Christ portrayed, it must be communal as well as educational. It must help us to integrate message and medium, to see that significance has to be set in its proper place alongside solidarity, to recognize that without interdependence, independence is simply self-centred, lonely and ultimately destructive. It is in its inability to offer any *collective* vision for the future that the Education Reform Act most clearly fails.

The vision of community, as with the kingdom, must be rooted in reality. Our 'vision managers' cannot be prophets who purvey pipe-dreams. We require those, deeply grounded in the trials and tribulations (as well as achievements and joys) of education as a communal experience and endeavour, to point the way forward. If ERA has given us anything, it is perhaps, by mistake rather than intention, an opportunity to shake clear of the dead weight of the past and begin to learn anew what real education is all about. For 'If you always do what you do, you'll only get what you've got.' Not exactly the words of Christ. But he certainly said something very like it.

REFERENCES

Berger, P. (1980) *The Heretical Imperative*. New York: Anchor Press, Doubleday.
Clark, D. (1987) *Yes to Life: In Search of the Kingdom Community*. London: Collins. (Fount Paperback).
Clark, D. (1989) *Community Education: Towards a Framework for the Future*. Birmingham: Westhill College.
Handy, C. and Aitken, R. (1986) *Understanding Schools as Organizations*. Harmondsworth: Penguin.
Newbigin, L. (1986) *Foolishness to the Greeks*. London: SPCK.
Palmer, P. (1977) *A Place Called Community*. Wallingford, Pennsylvania: Pendle Hill Publications.

Chapter 13

Active Citizenship: A Rationale for the Education of Citizens?

Garth Allen

The debate about the nature of citizenship is fundamentally a debate about what kind of society we want to live in and the role of education in achieving this. Recent interest in the concept of the 'Active Citizen' reflects an attempt at the remoralization of society. It is premised upon a particularistic and exclusive model of human virtue and a highly politicized view of education. Having examined the emergent, and now somewhat shaky, orthodoxy of the 1980s and its context in policy, Garth Allen proceeds to argue the case for an alternative conception of citizenship which is located within a quite different tradition of political education. This insists that a defensible rationale for educating the citizen for a free and democratic society must 'require the possibility and assume the probability of dissent'. Such an education aims to produce a politically literate citizen who understands the scope for 'personal independence' within a wider framework of 'communal obligation'. The state is instrumental in creating the conditions in which the dissenting citizen can be educated.

INTRODUCTION

In the 1980s, the UK subjected itself to intense national criticism fuelled by the anguish of perceived economic and moral decline. The political and popular response was to affirm this decline and seek its resolution through reinventing perceived successful decades as Golden Ages, as images of an ideal present. Individuals such as Richard Branson, Princess Diana and Sebastian Coe became virtuous role models. Other countries, such as Japan and Germany, were held up to reflect the social and private benefits which accrue to well-regulated hard work and ambition. This soul-searching is a major outcome of collective and individual political opinion. Political consciousness, its form and degree, is largely determined by opinions about how well off we feel we are in relation to our views about how well off we deserve to be.

This chapter aims to show how causes and solutions to social issues manifest themselves in the UK through examining the debate about Active Citizenship, its role both as a flashing red indicator for the British disease and as a rallying cry for the rectification of past and present ills.

One of the dominant images to emerge from the Conservative Party in the late 1980s was the model of human virtue enshrined within the term 'Active Citizen'. The former

Home Secretary, Douglas Hurd, told the Conservative Party Conference in October 1988 that 'the game of dodging responsibility, of passing the parcel of blame from one group to another, simply has to stop'.

Whatever happened to the active citizen? So asked a *Guardian* reader in April 1990. He might well ask. These buzzwords of the late 1980s have seemingly disappeared without trace. However, I shall propose that there is a process of evolution whereby the Active Citizen of necessity frequently becomes a dissident citizen. The clearest example of this was over the question of the poll tax, which brought violence back on the streets and helped bring the Tory Party to the brink of defeat.

Taking responsibility for one's own actions and their consequences is an aim of education which many have subscribed to. In what ways and to what extent, if any, should moulding this Active Citizen be a priority of present-day education? The argument which follows is that central government has confused the distinction between education and indoctrination by allowing one image of the Active Citizen to emerge and to dominate public discourse (Brennan, 1981). This, as we shall see, is one example of the dangers of majority rule, since the legitimacy of such propaganda has been located in the ballot box or in the public mandate given through four consecutive 'votes of confidence' for a single-party government. An alternative image to the AC (Active Citizen) will be introduced, the DC (Dissenting Citizen), and the thin dividing line which exists between the two will be traced.

Current New Right ideology underwrites the reaffirmation of national strength, identity and pride. Mrs Thatcher's personal achievement in reaching world statemanship reflected the degree of success of this overriding goal of political strategy. Avoiding the negation of this success – actual or perceived economic decline – has been largely achieved through a remoralization of the British people so that they will have what Mrs Thatcher claimed they have always wanted, freedom to be significant wealth producers for themselves and their families.

The dismantling and dramatic restructuring of the public sector economic and welfare states, criticized as neither seeking nor achieving efficiency and accountability, derive their initial strength and gather momentum from the popular, ballot box applause for the model of human virtue underwriting such goals and policies, writ large as the Active Citizen.

National progress has frequently been charted as a victory for classes or groups who have wrested concessions from the state to create an increasingly extended and enlightened society. The state has accepted a responsibility for ensuring that its people are not debarred from Active Citizenship by being too poor, too ill, too ignorant or too apathetic. The New Right claims that this paternalistic approach represents restrictions on human freedoms by transferring income or services to people who, as a result of being brought above the level of destitution, become the slave-like dependants of the state.

Active Citizens are free citizens but within a clear, strict moral order. Active Citizens will not be truly free to take responsibility for their own actions unless the state guarantees that they will never be called on to support individuals or causes which no human – other than a saint – would reasonably be expected to support. Active Citizens will be freed from the forced requirement to transfer resources, via the state, to the undeserving poor. The proper restricted role of the state is to enable free market forces to work unfettered by restrictive practices and to enable Active Citizens to accumulate wealth and to monopolize other scarce experiences – fresh air, clean beaches, great opera, museums and art galleries and even soccer matches. The state is reducing its economic interference to the minimal level necessary to ensure this. At the same time it will do as much as needs to be done in order to ensure that the emerging army of wealth creators, free from the dead hand of public ownership and legal and financial regulation, will willingly dispense some proportion of the fruits of their new freedom to the deserving poor. The welfare state has to be rolled back, restructured and targeted towards enabling the moral obligations of charity, philanthropy and altruism to break free from the suffocation of state paternalism. Active Citizens will take increased responsibility for wealth creation simultaneously to produce a stronger nation and a stronger economy, bonding people together within and between families in a new moral order.

Neal Ascherson has identified a nasty underside to Active Citizenship (*Observer*, 10 October 1988):

> The neighbour who writes anonymous denunciations to the police, the passenger who draws the guard's attention to another passenger who might be travelling first class on a second class ticket, the French concierge who tells a returning husband about the men who visited his wife; these too are active citizens who exist in all countries. Active citizens provided the Gulag Archipelago with much of its population.

John Dewey (1916), as usual, helps us to cue in the educational dimension:

> The concept of education as a social process and function has no definite meaning until we define the kind of society we have in mind.

Should we create an educational environment which matches the kind of society Douglas Hurd had in mind when he popularized the virtues of Active Citizens? John Dewey would not, I suspect, have followed the Hurd instinct, nor followed Mrs Thatcher. Mrs Thatcher, writes Peter Kellner (*Independent*, 17 October 1988) was 'engaged in the political equivalent of genetic engineering', redefining the words we use to define Britain's political landscape, 'a breathtaking venture, as important as cutting taxes or privatising utilities'. Active Citizens would be passive citizens who uncritically or unintentionally subscribe to the only vision of human virtue recommended.

Citizenship is to do with belonging, to becoming a member. Membership of a nation is paradoxically seen as the legitimate stamp of individuality – in particular, being British. Our citizens abroad – soccer supporters, tourists, overseas sales managers – expect their 'Britishness' to be acknowledged, and, if necessary, put into battle as a counter to the laws and conventions of other countries. However, the concept of Britishness must be susceptible to continuous review and reformulation within a genuine representative democracy. Freedom of speech and association, principles of one-person-one-vote and constant countervailing power, require the possibility and assume the probability of dissent. Images of Active Citizens in a healthy and genuine representative democracy should proliferate and the resolution of conflicts arising from alternative preferences concerning the good life should be an essential function of government. Governments must reflect a majority version of the good life but, unlike in totalitarian states, this majority version must not be imposed on a depoliticized, uncritical electorate.

THE BRITISH DEBATE ABOUT ACTIVE CITIZENSHIP, 1988–1990

The concept

Douglas Hurd, when Home Secretary, developed the Tory commitment to define citizenship in 1988 as a policy ploy to defy Opposition attempts to equate conservatism with material self-interest. The concept contains a vision of citizens as those people who, if unshackled from the paternalistic welfare state, would freely engage in acts of altruism, philanthropy and charity. Voluntary and charitable organizations would flourish and reveal people's true nature, their natural empathy and concern for others. This vision also served to offset Mrs Thatcher's oft-quoted remarks concerning the absence of society. Active citizenship offers a reinterpretation of this claim, stressing that processes of mutual aid are doomed to wither away if these are imposed and over-regulated by the state.

In May 1990 John Patten, then Home Office Minister of State, reaffirmed the positive rather than negative role of the Active Citizen image (Patten, 1990):

> To argue that the active citizen is a by-product of a prosperous community troubled by its conscience is patently wrong. Voluntary work, concern for a neighbour, and simple human kindness are not driven by exchange rates, money supply or mortgage interest rates. To suggest that they are is to turn a blind eye to known facts about charitable giving and volunteering. It is also to assign a spurious importance to the economy as a determinant of behaviour. Active citizenship has already fired the imagination of many people and I am convinced that the 1990s will see this develop into a powerful third force in our country. In my view an active citizen is someone making more than a solely economic contribution to his or her community, someone who not only cares but who also acts on their caring instincts.

Mr Patten developed the idea further than Douglas Hurd. Patten claimed that the private sector ought to see the emergence of 'Active Businesses'. These businesses support voluntary work through secondment of staff, promote volunteering on in-house pre-retirement courses, write cheques for charities and sporting activities and generally are aware 'that their responsibilities extend beyond their immediate workforce to the community'.

Mr Hurd frequently returned to his theme. In 1989, in a speech in Honiton, Devon, he introduced a further elaboration, the concept of 'good stewardship'. This notion was directed towards those responsible for the delivery of public services and was itself derived from the theme of a 1989 address to the Audit Commission by John Major, then Chief Secretary to the Treasury. The common political concern was that Conservatives should not be portrayed as hostile to efficient public sector providers. The role offered to doctors, headteachers and police superintendents by Mr Hurd and Mr Major was that they cannot avoid direct responsibility for people in their care; the buck stops with them.

Active citizenship remains part of the Conservative Party lexicon with no strong counter-proposition currently available. Two distinguished academics and social commentators and activists, Ralf Dahrendorf and Professor David Marquand, have analysed this 'big idea' of Active Citizenship (*Guardian*, 1 and 15 August 1990). For Dahrendorf, citizenship is a system of rights or entitlements, constitutionally guaranteed to all members of society. These rights should be social, political, economic and legal. This concept does not sit easily with market forces, which accentuate the 'Two

Nations' division, as Marquand also points out, 'creating an under-class cut off from political participation by social deprivation'. Rights, of course, for Douglas Hurd, are only legitimated if matched by duties. Indeed, this is another dominant layer of meaning within Active Citizenship. Both Dahrendorf and, though to a lesser extent, Marquand are appalled by this formulation. As Dahrendorf says: 'There is something extraordinarily unpleasant in the spectacle of well-heeled Thatcherites or Reaganites egging their leaders on to further attacks on the worn fabric of global entitlement on the grounds that too much is heard of rights these days and not enough of duties.' The Active Citizen for Dahrendorf is a feature of totalitarianism since the obligations are those of a loyal and dutiful subject acting out a single political image. Active citizens do not have those obligations to the preservation and extension of rights which, according to Dahrendorf, are a feature of free citizens of a democratic state. Robespierre, Stalin and Pol Pot would happily live with the concept. More recently, it seems easy to equate the emergence of a big idea such as Active Citizenship with the growth of political and religious fundamentalism in the UK. Paradoxically, fundamentalism is an assertion of the right to be different.

Political consciousness

What are the dominant political values in Britain today? The ultimate success of any attempt to establish a political system based on icons such as the Active Citizen or universal citizenship (as with Charter 88) depends upon the extent to which the moral climate for a new culture of citizenship can be created. How do values such as the enterprise culture, moral vigilante, voluntary obligation, civic virtue and a 'sense of community' fit with what people actually believe in?

One recent analysis by Richard Rose and Ian McAllister (1990) suggests that there are new forms of value groups which replace older divisions of Right and Left. The Right now split between those favouring a free market in everything but sexual and family morality and nationalism and what they call a social market group which retains a major role for the welfare state. The left divide between Hard Left and Soft Left. All share provision and welfare values but the Hard Left is also against institutionalized authority (in the school, home and through the police). They argue that voters now cluster into nine different value groups (see Figure 13.1).

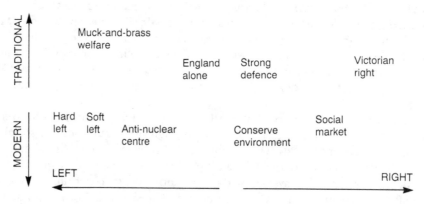

Figure 13.1   Nine different value groups of voters.

Some people seem to be well on the road to Active Citizenship. In a survey in January 1990 of young people aged 16–24 and *not* at school, in Further Education or Higher Education, seven distinct groups were identified (*Euromonitor*, 1990):

'Life's a party' (20 per cent of sample)   Enjoyment seekers, Tory voters, lager drinkers with little ambition and less social responsibility. A hangover from the 1980s, they are racist and anti-homosexual and are concentrated in the 18–20 age group in the South East.

'Safety seekers' (18 per cent)   Labour voting but middle-of-the-road, with unexceptional tastes and habits. Notably nervous of flying and of using the Channel tunnel, they are prominent in the 22–24 age range in the Midlands.

'Outsiders' (18 per cent)   The remaining idealists, they are alienated from authority and incline towards Labour or Green politics. With low income, they buy their clothes from market stalls and, despite claiming to live for holidays, take few of them.

'New moralists' (14 per cent)   Austere, cautious and clean-living, they are against drinking and smoking and in favour of keeping fit. One in four would vote Green. Likely to live alone.

'Authoritarians' (14 per cent)   They are bigoted and aggressive. Two in three are women and they include the highest proportion of supporters of the Social Democrat Party. Pro-police, they drink gin and tonic, vodka and Malibu.

'Greying youths' (8 per cent)   Middle-aged before their time, they prefer cash to cheques or credit cards, are keen on marriage and would rather spend an evening in front of the television than go to a concert. Pro-Labour, they are numerous in the 22–24 age group in Lancashire and Yorkshire.

'Young moderates' (8 per cent)   The softer face of the 1990s, they are pro-Labour, family-oriented and more celibate than any other group. With low incomes, they buy clothes from catalogues and like cycling.

Educational policy

Another survey, by the School of Education at the University of Leicester, examined citizenship education in 455 secondary schools. This survey was commissioned by The Speaker's Commission on Citizenship, set up under Bernard Weatherill, Speaker of the House of Commons, in 1989. The main conclusion drawn from the survey by its Chairman, Mr Maurice Stonefrost, was that: 'Young people are leaving school without a clear idea of their rights and responsibilities as citizens' (*Guardian*, 21 January 1990). A submission from the Commission was made to the National Curriculum Council. The main approach appears to have been to arrive at a standard syllabus (given the wide variation in citizenship studies shown by the survey) itself governed by a definition of citizenship. The concept, as elaborated at a February 1990 citizenship conference addressed by the Prince of Wales, is deceptively broad. It includes caring for relatives as well as a willingness and ability to join controversial single-issue campaign groups. However, the most interesting feature of the Commission's work has been its interest in and insistence on young people having the opportunity to complete a nationally recognized community service course. There is already, of course, extensive charity fundraising in schools as well as community service and public service work experience programmes (see 'Volunteering' below).

Further unanimity about citizenship education displayed itself at the February

Speaker's Conference. The then Education Secretary, John MacGregor, and his Labour shadow, Jack Straw, both agreed that pupils should be *trained* in citizenship. This training should include the teaching of individual duties and responsibilities (no mention of Dahrendorf's rights), respect for the law and training to understand how society works. Neither, I suspect, would want pupils to serve an apprenticeship with Bruce Kent, Arthur Scargill or Edwina Currie.

These views exist within a broader and deeply divided debate on education policy. Current educational policy is derived from broad conservative themes (not all exclusive to the Tories) such as teachers and local government being the problem rather than the solution to raising educational standards and claiming the low educational standards of teachers and pupils to be the cause of moral and economic decline. Of particular interest to the Active Citizenship concept was Mrs Thatcher's personal involvement in the evolution of a standard history syllabus for the secondary school core curriculum. Her stress on English history, facts and progress seems derived from and limited by the Hurd and Patten visions of citizens as *de facto* fundamentalists.

Volunteering

We now know quite a lot about people's views about voluntary work and volunteering. Indeed, recent surveys by Mori Poll and Social and Community Planning Research (Volunteer Centre, 1990), suggest that the 1988–1990 drive to promote Active Citizenship may well fail to deliver because of the crucial importance of voluntary – i.e. free – activity within the concept and the apparent negative image of voluntary work. Volunteers are still seen as Richard Briers characters, middle-class, middle-brow and meddling where they are not wanted. People tend not to volunteer because of the fear of being pressed to do more and more, because it costs them money to do so and because they do not like asking other people for money or goods.

The Prince of Wales is a well-known advocate of volunteering. His National Volunteer Force, established in 1990, offers people aged 16–24 the chance to participate in voluntary projects. The government has given £50 000 pump-priming money to it. Its central idea, according to the Prince, is to encourage people to mix together for a joint purpose. These Charlie's Angels will be largely funded by Training Schemes, employers, the Prince's Trust and the voluntary sector itself. Young people in work, in education or on the dole will be encouraged to spend twelve to eighteen weeks full- or part-time on projects including helping the disabled, elderly and mentally handicapped. The Prince hopes that the scheme will give its participants a new sense of community (displacing the old or filling a void?) and guide potential which might otherwise be misdirected. It does not sound as if the 'life's a party' group will be the first to sign on.

Calor Gas too is associated with the Active Citizen concept. It sponsors an award organized by the National Federation of Women's Institutes, which plans to find the 'Citizen of the '90s'. The panel of judges is WI Chair Jean Varnam, who, in a press release (*Western Evening Herald*, 2 February 1990) explained the WI's reason for launching the competition (open, incidentally, to women and men):

> This new award highlights our role as a dynamic organization addressing the social issues of the '90s as we celebrate 75 years of WI service to the community at grassroots level. Citizenship plays a vital part in combating the pressures placed upon communities by the

ever increasing pace of modern life. As a community-based organisation we believe it is time that a major award scheme recognised those unsung heroes who make such a valuable contribution to the lives of so many in this country.

This competition is but one feature of the spread of volunteering and its role in the restructuring of local government and local services. 'Active Businesses', as we have seen, may well control the agenda of voluntary groups (Calor Gas over the WI?) as a direct result of funding them. This funding may well go to largely uncontroversial bodies, such as the WI, the NSPCC and Telethons. This will reduce funding to less glamorous voluntary groups (Shelter, Gingerbread, local Family Centres). What is happening is that the voluntary sector itself is fast becoming inseparable from the new private sector culture. Hurd and Patten Active Citizens will be equally at home in ICI and War on Want. In both, management and public relations issues have displaced consumer sovereignty as the main decision-making force.

Trickle-down wealth

Should poor people support the establishment of a New Model Army of Active Citizens? European Commission research indicates that the number of people who blame poverty on injustice has almost doubled since 1976. Seventy per cent of people believe that the government is not doing enough to help the poor and 41 per cent agree that the poor have 'almost no chance'. The Commission polled a sample of 12 000 people in the twelve EC states. Fifty per cent said they would be willing to give up 'a little money' to help the poor (*Guardian*, 5 June 1990).

Active Citizens would be wealth and income maximizers who would then freely (rather than involuntarily through progressive taxation) choose to disperse some of their resources to the deserving poor. In the EC survey, when asked which of two statements best reflected their view of society, 80 per cent chose 'the rich get richer and the poor get poorer', while only 12 per cent opted for 'there is less and less difference in income between the rich and the poor'.

Even health authorities in the UK are having to appeal to trickle-down theories of resource redistribution. *The Guardian* (19 April 1990) reported that the West Sussex Health Authority has appealed to local residents and businesses for basic revenue finance. A charitable trust has been set up in Worthing, to be administered by the Woolwich Building Society, to help the 1700 patients in the district who have been waiting for over a year for their operations. This is the first time a health authority has appealed to local residents and businesses for basic revenue finance. This shift arises directly out of Mrs Thatcher's oft-quoted exhortation: 'When you have finished as a tax payer, you have not finished your duty as a citizen.' The Charities Aid Foundation annual surveys of the level of charitable donations made by individuals in the UK show an average of 10p per week per person.

In a Commons debate on Active Citizenship and voluntary organizations in December 1989, it was the Tory MP for Wimbledon, Dr Charles Goodrow-Wicker, who claimed that increased private prosperity (i.e. via tax cuts) must be linked with taking greater responsibility for others. John Patten, once more playing a central role in nurturing the Active Citizen concept, criticized Labour-controlled councils: 'I am sad to say that there are areas . . . where it is extremely difficult to be an active citizen working in the teeth of local opposition.' Once again, we see the theme of setting people free from collective agreements and organizations in order that they will, through human nature, wish voluntarily to redistribute resources.

POLITICAL EDUCATION AND ACTIVE CITIZENSHIP

Political education in a representative democracy encompasses any educational process which encourages and enables people to understand the personalization of the political in their lives and the politicization of the personal. It enables them to make judgements about the distribution of power and resources unravelled in this understanding and to effect changes in these power and resource holdings if these do not fit a rational image of the good life or of human virtue. Politically educated people would be able and willing in a representative democracy to protect themselves and others from the abuse of power and the associated unwarranted loss of freedoms. They would be able to protect themselves and others from inequalities in the distribution of income and wealth and other valued possessions. The trouble with the Hurd Active Citizen is that it is put forward as the only model which reasonable people would aspire to for themselves and defend as a personal goal for others to achieve. Kenneth Baker, when Education Secretary, made this quite clear in his use of categorical language in a speech at Bolton School, an opting out school, in Lancashire.

> Deploring 'moral ambiguities, '60s attitudes to let it all hang out, and the four-letter word', the Minister suggested the only four-letter word which 'trendy parents' shrank from using was 'don't'. (*Guardian*, 10 November 1988)

He went on to describe social scientists as the

> handmaidens of a revolution in which concepts of right and wrong have become blurred. There are moral values and concepts of right and wrong which are classless, universal, and essential, and which we can all share irrespective of background, religion, or political belief.

Children, according to Mr Baker, should be taught that it was wrong to lie, steal, cheat, and bully; and right to respect your elders, to know that you cannot have everything you want instantly, to take responsibility for your actions: 'Above all it is right to help those less fortunate and those weaker than ourselves.'

Any democracy should be able to ensure that its citizens are able to lead autonomous lives of their own choosing as morally responsible individuals. This moral responsibility is learnt through attempting to achieve considered, reflective choices on the type of life to live. Mary Warnock (1979), prior to and in contrast to Mr Baker, argued in 1974 that schools should timetable periods of silence and reflection. Reflecting needs something to reflect on and a representative democracy, built on the probability of significant political change, should, through its educational system, offer people alternative concepts of the good life. How else are we to ensure that one version is not arbitrarily imposed? Robert Nozick (1974) raised libertarian or Utopian thinking above the slur of anarchy and recovered the crucially important claim that Utopia exists when we are all free and able and willing to visualize and work to realize our preferred choice of Utopia.

Utopian thinking connects with democratic theory at the point where it is claimed that no conception of the good life can be arbitrarily imposed on anyone and no one should be subject to arbitrary interference. Neighbourhood Watch schemes would be seen to be antithetical to these principles. What arguably a representative democracy should have is a range of alternative conceptions of Active Citizenship with the caveat that these can be limited to democratic forms if it is accepted that there is no morally preferable political system to democracy. Education in a democratic society means delineating the features of Active Citizenship which make the concept democratic, accepting that there will be different ideal types and different education arrangements which are congruent with these ideal types.

One Dissenting Citizen profile, firmly locked into a representative democratic tradition, was drawn up by the co-directors of the Nuffield Foundation-funded National Programme for Political Education, 1974–77, located in the twin centres of London (Birkbeck College, with Bernard Crick) and York (Department of Education, University of York, with Ian Lister). The opening paragraph of the first major working paper of the project gives a clear view of the Dissenting Citizen (Crick and Lister, 1974):

> Many people are not politically literate, perhaps we should *not* say 'politically illiterate'. Some may be politically effective, but that is not quite the same thing: unconscious habits can sometimes make one politically effective, as may in other circumstances fanatical intensity. Or a passive and deferential population, who think of themselves as good subjects and not *active citizens*, or who do not think of politics at all, may for some purposes pose few problems to the carrying on of government. But 'political literacy' involves both some conscious understanding of what one is about in a given situation and some capacity for action.

Bernard Crick was adamant that a representative or liberal democracy requires a citizenry willing and able to choose between alternative political parties and groups. In turn, Ian Lister, influenced by John Dewey's work, emphasized the need to avoid the elitism of the reactionary Black Papers of the late 1960s and early 1970s and the off-putting romanticism and nihilism of deschooling.Lister was concerned about the extent to which schools could be democratic, could teach about democracy and teach for democracy. Both Crick and Lister wished to test the boundaries of tolerance by examining whether an educational theory whose goal was the creation of politically active citizens could be implemented in public sector schools and colleges. Politically literate citizens would avoid slipping into an unconscious deference and would possess the potential for dissent.

> Political literacy must be a compound of knowledge, skills and attitudes, to be developed together, each conditioning the other. Knowledge alone was rejected as an object of political education, but so was an unreflective and uninformed participation.

A politically literate person would significantly participate in political life not out of duty but from free choice. In asserting, specifying and promoting political literacy, Crick and Lister were always clear that they were not 'postulating some universal role or model: different politically literate persons might have a number of characteristics which vary one from another'. Equally,

> It would be wrong to define a politically literate person as someone who necessarily shares the values of Western European liberalism. That would be, indeed, a curious up-dating of the Whig interpretation of history into present day political education. Such views are to be learned as part of our tradition, but they must themselves be subject to criticism, some scepticism must be part of any citizen and of any worthwhile education, and they must not be universalised without the utmost self-awareness, self-criticism and thought for consequences. However, it is clear, at the least, that there are some kinds of political effectiveness

which simply destroy the possibility of other kinds of political literacy. Some biases are compatible with a true knowledge of the motives, beliefs and behaviour of others, some not. Functional political literacy may well be imposed and narrowing. All values are not equal.

Within any form of democracy, the Dissenting Citizen would possess the attributes necessary and sufficient to dissent from the imposition of an orthodoxy, to be able to turn the failure of indoctrination into an educational opportunity.

The relationship between democratic theories and political education practices was never fully developed in the published texts and papers of the Project (but see White, 1983). However, the successful application for funding reflected a critique of capitalist elite democracies. Habermas has argued that the power structure of capitalist economies requires a depoliticized population reinforced by the competitive materialism and welfare state paternalism which 'cools out' potential dissent. The National Programme for Political Education never claimed this form of ideological justification for its existence – that is, to overcome depoliticization – but it did share and use a fear of depoliticization in order to obtain funding. Lord Trend, a prominent Nuffield Trustee and former Permanent Secretary to the Cabinet, subsequently Rector of Lincoln College, Oxford, was dismayed at the political disaffection and low level of interest in politics that applicants to his college displayed. Low turnouts at central and local elections, opinion poll evidence concerning distrust or dislike of politicians and the falling membership of political parties showed that Oxford applicants were part of a general pattern which illustrated the lack of interest and trust in a political system that required people to exercise their vote willingly (there being no legal obligation) and intelligently. One characteristic of being politically literate would be to choose to vote after due consideration or to choose to create alternative democratic processes and structures. The National Programme for Political Education, an *educational* research and development project, was a major response to the perceived failings of a political system of representative democracy and a capitalist economic system. A willingness and ability to engage in political action led the Project team beyond an implied critique of representative democracy into a debate about whether it was possible and desirable to educate *for* a participatory democracy and to educate through educational institutions congruent with the vision of a participatory democracy (Pateman, 1970). The politically literate person, as an active citizen, would clearly need to be a Dissenting Citizen in order to work for the realization of an alternative democratic political system to representative democracy, and an alternative economic system to capitalism. Is it currently possible to educate *for* dissent as well as *about* dissent?

> A politically literate person must be able to use his knowledge, or at least see how it could be used and have a proclivity for using it, but equally his or her desire to participate must be informed by as much knowledge of what he is going into and of what consequences are likely to follow from his actions as is needed to make participation effective and justifiable. (Crick and Lister, 1974)

One feature of such an education process is clear: it would be sharply distinguished from indoctrination. Indeed, the training of teachers and youth workers might, once more, have to include courses and experiences which enable teachers to identify and suppress in themselves or deny in others indoctrination. CATE criteria for teacher training leave little time for such luxuries. Similarly, HMI reports on teacher training courses stress the need for subject studies plus classroom management skills plus economic awareness and little else. Indoctrination would be characterized by teaching from images of virtuous people and the good life as if these were the only images available while simultaneously ensuring, through controlling the agenda of the lesson, the progression of the course and the salient features of the hidden curriculum, so that no counter-visions emerged. Clever, sensitive teachers can enable people to give equal consideration to a range of Utopias, including their own, while leaving the student free. Indoctrination would imprint an arbitrary conception of the good life as if it were a universal truth.

Pat White (1983) has developed the detail of the relationships between education, indoctrination and democracy more than any other British philosopher in recent years. First, she claims, we should accept that in a democracy there are no moral experts on the good life for individuals to follow in detail (Sir William Rees-Mogg not excepted!). The only authority is that which clearly rests on the considered, sensitive choice of an individual able and willing to reflect on possible lives. She shares with Fred Inglis (1985) the view that educated people would not live in the ghetto of restricted imagination. Politically literate people, we need to add, would be sensitive to the nature and extent of indoctrinatory forces in order to choose whether to turn indoctrination into education. (Not all indoctrination is bad; for example, to indoctrinate to avoid committing certain criminal or dangerous activities might be desirable.)

Second, argues Pat White, we should acknowledge the extraordinary agreement about what counts as human progress. The Dissenting Citizen would be a disturbing concept if it implied continuous dissent. But this is neither necessary nor likely. The agreement Pat White is referring to is that in liberal democracies there is the implicit acknowledgement that governments should guarantee those goods and services and freedoms which are the prerequisites for both living a good life, recognizing or imagining different conceptions of the good life, and ensuring that citizens are tolerant of these differences. The absence of poverty, ignorance, hunger and ill health are the necessary conditions which underpin the exercise of political imagination and political strategy. Yet there is the danger that the new Active Citizens are people who, as never before in post-war Britain, can demonstrate that they deserve their citizenship partly through identifying and clamouring (fuelled by the popular press) for the punishment of dissent. These state guaranteed rights and entitlements to a minimal good life remain only for the deserving Active Citizens. The current buzz welfare policy phrases of 'targeted groups' and 'value for money' reflect the view that Active Citizens, through transfer payments and subsidies and the finance of welfare state institutions and professions, have been trapped by an unfair universal redistribution system which rewards the bad as well as the good.

Procedural values congruent with the moral frameworks of participatory democracies also need to be spelt out. Critics of the possibility of ever realizing a participatory democracy have argued that the concept itself is contrary to human nature; many people, it is claimed, while experiencing only the conditional satisfaction of representative government, would not swap it for any other system. This may or may not be true. The Dissenting Citizen would wish to reflect, at least, on the possibility. A Dissenting Citizen would have the confidence and feelings of efficacy to override deference, servility and acquiescence. From the past, from other countries or from the imagination would come possible Utopias which would need to be worked out in detail – no small task!

The Crick and Lister (1974) specification of political literacy is quite clear about the crucial although partial role of imagination:

> A politically literate person would also know the kinds of knowledge that he or she needed, and did not possess, in a given situation, and how to find them out. Paradoxically, the politically literate person knows what he or she does not know.

Bernard Crick (1975) was equally clear about the need for and nature of these procedural values:

> If there is a genuine political education, certain values are presupposed. I will call these procedural values for they are not substantive values like various justifications of authority, like *equality* or types of *justice*, but rather presuppositions of any kind of genuine political education or free political activity. For one thing, the politically literate person cannot just accept one set of values as correct: he will see that the very nature of politics lies in there being a plurality of values and interests, of which he must have at least some minimal understanding.

In paragraph 6 of Document 1 of the Programme for Political Education these procedural values were boldly and simply identified as 'freedom, toleration, fairness, respect for truth and respect for reasoning' (Crick, 1975).

> I assume that a teacher should not ordinarily seek to influence the substantive values of pupils – and that frontal assaults are not likely, in any case, to be successful. But I assume that it is proper and possible to nurture and strengthen these procedural values. Anyone can see that in real life and politics there are many occasions when these values may have to be modified, because they can conflict with each other, or with substantive values such as religious, ethical and political doctrines embody. Part of political education is to examine just such conflicts. But this does not in any way affect the primacy of these procedural values within a genuine political education. The objection to them is, indeed, more likely to be that they are pie more than poison, nebulous platitudes more than harsh indoctrinatory concepts.

It remains to specify the forms of power relationships with which a Dissenting Citizen would wish to flourish in order to create and maintain genuine democratic political systems. The claim is that this virtuous person, the politically literate or Dissenting Citizen, would be aware of a range of power forms that need to be prioritized according to rational thought within the moral framework of the procedural values. Political action, the key educated outcome of political education as we have defined it, requires the defensible use of power.

Pat White (1983) argues for an education *in* power and claims that we should recognize that power lies within those institutions which determine the distribution of income and then analyse what income does and does not buy. She claims that within a participatory democracy, citizens would prefer as egalitarian a distribution of political and economic power as was consistent with ensuring an appropriate division of labour. Furthermore, she maintains that citizens would want the state to ensure a level of welfare provision below which no one must be allowed to fall.

White's exercise in guesswork or logic is familiar, though no less important for that. However, the forms of power are still left unspecified through these claims about the preferences of power holders. What forms of power may DCs legitimately use to arrive at this egalitarian Utopia, should they choose to work for it? Forms of power can be categorized in many ways (e.g. see Wilkinson, 1986), including the spectrums of violent–non-violent, coercion–persuasion, education–indoctrination, manipulation–openness, argument–brainwashing. Each of these is itself conditioned by the source of authority vested in the power holder. Active Citizens are energetic wealth creators for self and family and for nation and community. Community is interpreted as an obligation, derived from celebration of the well-being that comes from material wealth, to dispense charity, philanthropy and altruism to the unhappy but deserving poor. The capacity to provide and the need to receive transfer payments and subsidies may be the most significant power relationship of our times, for such payments determine the nature and extent of dependency relationships and thereby define the limits of personal independence and communal obligation, and, hence, freedom from arbitrary interference. As Crick and Lister (1974) state:

> An understanding of politics must begin with an understanding of the conflicts that there are and of the reasons and interests of the contestants; it cannot be content with preconceptions of constitutional order or of a necessary consensus. A politically literate person will not hope to resolve all such differences, or all differences at once; but he perceives their very existence as politics.

The claim must now be directly made that the politically literate person is the Dissenting Citizen who may choose the Hurd image of the Active Citizen but who would be free to reject it and work for alternative visions of human virtue and the good life. Dissenting people may disagree with a prevalent or official view. Dissent comes from the prior quality of resistance and a politically literate person would only knowingly acquiesce to any prevailing orthodoxy. We need to reassert the educational implications of the 1970s Programme for Political Education in a form which connects with the immediate future. Current state policies and proposals are stuck together with the super-glue of indoctrination such that the materialist moralists and eclectic elitists of the New Right and the institutional conservatism of socialism are difficult to challenge.

A right to equal treatment and respect is a necessary condition for the expression of dissent without fear of reprisal or disqualification from civil society. As long as governments legitimize inequalities and orthodoxy, the educational focus for producing the Dissenting Citizen has to be on education *for* human rights. This would at least set the agenda for ensuring the guarantee of minimal material inequalities in primary goods such as income, health, learning and self-respect, a guarantee which the Butskellite consensus of the post-war years acknowledged but failed to deliver, a guarantee which has now been expired for more than a decade. George Orwell, the creator of Winston Smith, is as pertinent today about the danger of totalitarianism as he was in 1949 (Wrong, 1979):

> Orthodoxy means not thinking – not needing to think. Orthodoxy is unconsciousness.

ACKNOWLEDGEMENT

Conversations with Richard Stewart, author and designer, were very helpful in shaping this chapter.

REFERENCES

Brennan, T. (1981) *Political Education in a Democracy*. London: Cambridge University Press.

Crick, B. (1975) 'Basic Concepts'. Document 3 of the Programme for Political Education.

Crick, B. and Lister, I. (1974) 'Political literacy: the centrality of the concept'. In B. Crick and A. Porter (eds) *Political Education and Political Literacy*. London: Longman.

Dewey, J. (1916) *Democracy and Education*. New York: Macmillan.

Inglis, F. (1985) *The Management of Ignorance*. Oxford: Basil Blackwell.

Nozick, R. (1974) *Anarchy, State and Utopia*. Oxford: Basil Blackwell.

Patten, J. (1990) In a speech to the Lions Club International Conference in Torquay.

Pateman, C. (1970) *Participation and Democratic Theory*. Cambridge: Cambridge University Press.

Rose, R. and McAllister, I. (1990) *The Loyalties of Voters: A Lifetime Learning Model*. London: Sage.

Voluntary Activity (1990) Volunteer Centre, Berkhamsted.

Warnock, M. (1979) *Schools of Thought*. London: Faber.

White, P. (1983) *Beyond Domination*. London: Routledge & Kegan Paul.

Wilkinson, P. (1986) *Terrorism and the Liberal State*. London: Macmillan.

Wrong, D. (1979) *Power: Its Forms, Bases and Uses*. Oxford: Basil Blackwell.

Young Britain: A Survey of Youth Culture in Transition (1990). London: Euromonitor.

Conclusion

Three general themes bind together the contributors to this book. First, they all claim that promoting education is a major part of their professional lives – yet few call themselves teachers. Second, all are sensitive to the setting that they meet their clients in and attempt to work from an active understanding and empathy for that setting; that is, they recognize community as a force in their work and accept the onus of being held accountable for the quality of social relationships which are introduced or changed as a result of their interventions. Third, they all have fears that the vision of the good life which underwrites their personal and professional being is seriously threatened by contemporary politics.

The main aim has been to allow practitioners to tell others about the politics that exists between the settings that configure professional interventions in the welfare state and a policy making, implementing and evaluating process which, to different degrees, responsible professionals have ambivalently created or instinctively resented. That is, beleaguered welfare state practitioners either work to sustain policy frameworks which they openly consider to be a hindrance rather than helpful, or their work reflects a professional acceptance of the system co-existing with a private condemnation. All have sought to reconstruct for positive alternatives to contemporary mainstream education and welfare policies using the contradictions and convergences of professional–lay relationships as the guide to personal and professional well-being. This politics of practice is about offering a private and public account of what is worth defending, whether this be the actual workings of a contemporary welfare practice or some vision of a preferred alternative – usually both co-exist, in creative or destructive tension.

Post-industrial society demands that practitioners identify, work to and defend – this cannot be avoided – their politics of practice and demands, too, that this politics will be broad enough and still strong enough to meet the needs of all people who have rights to be treated as citizens. This means that deriving a working concept of politics from a political movement will not be adequate since this will inevitably lead to felt exclusion by actual or potential clients who, in a culturally diverse society, have no need or wish to meet imperialism or partisanism in their dealings with welfare professionals. On the other hand, clients do expect their rights to equal treatment and respect to be sustained by commitment. We have to find a way forward beyond the poverty of old ideologies and the self-doubts of personal competence and personality. This becomes especially difficult when the dominant political agenda is largely antithetical to public-sector codes of practice and ways of working and when the dominant cultural rallying cry is for self-knowledge and self-confidence.

The politics of everyday life for welfare practitioners in the 1990s should be character-ized by a singular belief in the value of the citizens they work for. Given the unifying role of education in the work of the practitioners of this book, this means establishing a set of principles for all educators which will sustain and enhance democracy in post-industrial society. Such principles are being currently imposed on compulsory schooling, through the National Curriculum, national standards and national training prescriptions for teachers. Education for democracy through a morally acceptable politics of practice is not enhanced by schooling using operant conditioning and propaganda (e.g. for nation-alism and homophobism).

Encouraging Citizenship (HMSO, 1990), the Report of the Commission on Citizen-ship, has a Foreword by the former Speaker of the House of Commons, the Right Honourable Bernard Weatherill:

> I believe citizenship, like anything else, has to be learned. Young people do not become good citizens by accident, any more than they become good nurses, or good engineers or good bus drivers or computer scientists.

The aim and objectives of the Commission were to define citizenship and to search for the means of rewarding good citizenship with public recognition of achievement. In a representative democracy, the usual test for good citizenship has been the careful, reflective use of the vote and the freedom of association (with others of like minds) and speech. More recently this has been reinforced through the notion of equality of rights to effective influence over political processes and outcomes. These rights should be claimed by people in their professional lives in order to establish a politics of practice which allows the possibility of reconstructing political agendas through democratic means in order to create a democratic social structure. Democratic social systems cannot for long survive the top-down imposition of visions of the common good where no genuine alternative concepts can be identified, nurtured and consolidated. The Speaker's Commission on Citizenship recognized that what it called 'organised institu-tional collectives' may continue to decline but that specific-issue pressure groups are likely to continue to proliferate – communities created out of adversity.

Welfare state professionals have their own community of adversity, formed by the fears of dismantling the public sector, local government and the civil service, but driven by the need to continually respond to their citizens' demands. The call for a 'body charged with the specific responsibility to document and research social, economic and educa-tional aspects of citizenship; to consider new legislation in relation to the rights and duties of citizenship; and to stimulate informal public discussion' (HMSO, 1990) is to be welcomed if this helps establish due process for resolving conflict and grievance and an equitable distribution of the things people are considered to be entitled to.

Education and community come together as pointers to a set of educational principles which guarantee equal respect for citizens, including new citizens (immigrants, 18-year-olds, released prisoners and bankrupts, the decertified insane). The existing dominant world view in the UK, as described by Ian Lister (1988), is Anglocentric, nationalistic, imperialist/paternalist and monocultural and assumes the superiority of British values. The introduction to this book mentions the ambivalence of rhetoric with practice in many professional settings, and the accounts which follow illustrate the energy and insight needed to achieve publicly defensible professional fulfilment (which may not be congruent with prevailing modes of staff appraisal).

The political use of community here is to provide a counter to the values Lister identifies. Community can be claimed when peaceful means are identified and practised to resolve differences about the use and abuse of power (personal, institutional and regional) and unfair distributions of resources. The acceptance of differences, of course, is the high mark of community since the major procedural values underwriting peaceful conflict resolution are toleration through empathy.

Preaching the primacy of a politics of practice which recognizes cultural diversity as the main setting and which offers citizenship rights as the main guarantee for democratic procedures between professional and client and for just outcomes sounds like empty rhetoric in the face of seemingly entrenched structural inequalities. Establishing major social institutions – schools, hospitals, factories and so on – which are simultaneously democratic and efficient and are seen to create socially useful goods and services would tackle the unfairness of social inequalities head on. Unfortunately, we seem unable to create such institutional frameworks; they are more likely to fail to deliver needed goods and services, waste public resources in so doing, and alienate their employees through requiring them to be party to the failure. Welfare state professionals have two types of blood giving life to their practice: one is coloured by an assessment of clients' needs, the other by an analysis of the means by which people's life situations change. The reason why the contributors to this book are anxious about maintaining and enhancing their work is that they recognize their power in determining the welfare of others. This is both the political and moral base of their work.

Power will inevitably be exercised in settings which allow the possibility of exploitation, self-promotion or undetected error perpetrated by professionals and clients. The final prescription for the politics of practice, then, is that we need an education about power which identifies and analyses structural inequalities, which develops the skills of exercising power, which enhances the peaceful resolution of differences and which recognizes the rights of citizens to equality of respect and treatment.

The introduction to this book spoke of resistance and the professional need, sometimes, to reconstruct the policy framework of employers; to reinterpret clients' definition of needs as misplaced; and to dive beneath the prevailing political culture (currently, of seeking national prestige via economic strength from setting new sights for British industry's owners, managers and workers). To resist effectively requires an understanding of prevailing and potential power forms and bases. The politics of practice requires a working knowledge of the main forms of power: force, manipulation, persuasion and authority (Wrong, 1979) and the skills to use or resist these forms of power. The bases of power resources, both individual and collective (as in the state), weight of numbers (majority–minority issues) and, generally, processes of agenda setting in any social situation need to be intuitively if not formally assessed and internalized into the dynamics of the workings of professional practice. All of this, which is no small task, needs to be learnt by professionals on the job with appropriate review and evaluation procedures, including staff appraisal.

Finally, the working out of the politics between policy and practice has consciously to outlaw non-democratic procedures and outcomes. The word democracy thrives in theory and practice. Yet, such are the wide variety of claims made upon it, that it has been suggested that the concept is not capable of effective use in serious political analysis (Lively, 1975). Nonetheless, most of us know when things are not democratic even if we have difficulty in defining what democracy is. Perhaps the key lesson which the accounts in this book offer is that, in a democracy, professionals have to work with their clients rather than work upon them, and have to avoid the abuse of power and connect with economic inequalities and cultural patternings in order to achieve genuine human development. This is the politics of everyday life for welfare professionals and their clients. It means bringing community and democracy together by working out a politics of practice through a collaborative process of reconstructing the meaning of workplace democracy in the welfare state.

REFERENCES

HMSO (1990) *Encouraging Citizenship*. Report of the Commission on Citizenship. London: HMSO.

Lister, I. (1988) 'Civic education for positive pluralism'. Department of Education Working Paper, University of York.

Lively, J. (1975) *Democracy*. Oxford: Basil Blackwell.

Wrong, D. (1979) *Power: Its Forms, Bases and Uses*. Oxford: Basil Blackwell.

Name Index

Acland, Mrs 14
Ainley, P. 21
Aird, E. 98
Aitken, R. 118
Allen, G. 10
Apple, M.W. 46
Armstrong, H. 23, 97, (Flynn *et al.*) 98
Arnstein, S.R. 51
Aronowitz, S. 1
Ascherson, N. 132
Association of Metropolitan Authorities (AMA) 88, 90
Audit Commission 87, 90, 91

Baker, Kenneth 59, 138
Ball, S.J. 1, 4, 29
Barker, B. 26
Baron, S. 2, 30
Baruch, G. 77
Bastiani, J. 10 (Allen *et al.*), 44, 51–2
Batten, E. 45
Beechey, V. 58
Beddoe, D. 10, 12
Bell, C. 107
Berger, P. 118
Birmingham City Council Education Department 3
Bishop, J. 108, 112, 114
Blunkett, David 93
Bobbe, B. 19
Bosanquet, B. 22
Bowman, M. 95
Branca, P. 12
Brennan, T. 131
Brighouse, T. 33
Brookfield, S. 10, 68
Bruce, A. 97
Bryan, B. 58
Bryant, I. 69
Butler, J. 12

Callely, E. (Phillips *et al.*) 18
Cambridgeshire County Council 3
Cann, R. 114
Caron, M. (Fletcher *et al.*) 19
Carr, E.H. 10
CCCS 22
Charles, Prince of Wales 135, 136
Chew, A.N. 13
Chew, D.N. 13
Clark, D. 125, 126
Clarke, Kenneth 78
Cohen, P. 62
Council for National Academic Awards (CNAA) 60
Cowperthwaite, P. 73
Cox, R. 99
Crick, B. 139, 140, 142, 143
Cullingford, C. 47, 51

Dadzie, S. (Bryan *et al.*) 64
Dahrendorf, R. 133–4, 136
Dale, R. 31, 46
David, M. 2, 53
Davie, R. (Phillips *et al.*) 18
Davin, A. 12
Davison, A. 13
Dawes, F. 11
Dawson, J. 13
Department of Education and Science (DES) 106
Department of Health and Social Security (DHSS) 78
Dewey, J. 22, 132, 139

Dodds, G. 10
Donovan, J. 84

Entwhistle, H. 107

Ferris, H.J. 11
Fletcher, C. 19, 67, 68
Flynn, P. 97, 98
Fogleman, K. 105
Foley, C. 13
Foster, L. 80
Fraser, B. (Springhall *et al.*) 11
Fraser, L. 69
Freire, P. 66, 68–9, 70, 73, 74, 76, 80, 116
Further Education Unit 67

George, V. 25
Gilroy, P. 4, 58, 63
Giroux, H.A. 1, 106, 109, 116
Goffman, E. 77
Goodrow-Whicker, Charles 137
Gordon, P. 58
Gramsci, A. 5, 108
Green, A. 46
Green, T.H. 22
Greig, N. 95, 99–100
Griffiths, R. 78
Groombridge, J. 75
Gyford, G. 91

Hambleton, R. 88, 89
Handy, C. 118
Hargreaves, D. 1, 79–80
Harrison, D. (Dodds *et al.*) 10
Harvey, B. 26
Hayek, F.A. 57
Hoare, M. (Springhall *et al.*) 11
Hoggett, P. 3, 31, 88, 108, 112, 114
Holledge, J. 13
Hughes, M. 15
Humphries, B. 63
Hurd, Douglas 131, 132, 136

Inglis, F. 141

Jacobs, M. (Johnston *et al.*) 67
Jeffs, T. 33, 107
Jenkins, D. 30
Jenkins, R. 30
Jesus Christ 121–2, 123, 126–7, 129
Johnson, A. 105
Johnson, C. (Flynn *et al.*) 97, 98
Johnson, R. 12
Johnston, R. 67, 68, 72, (Cowperthwaite *et al.*) 73, 74, 75
Jonathan, R. 31, 50, 53
Jones, D. 22

Keeble, R.W.J. 15
Kellner, P. 132
Kennedy, M. 15
Keys, D. 95
King's Fund 80
Klug, F. 58
Knasel, E.G. 67

Lancashire Polytechnic 61
Lavender, P. 84
Lawrenson, Mrs 14
Le Grand, J. 31

149

Subject Index

Access courses 159–64
Accountability 28
Actionsport 113
Active Citizen movement 106, 130–43
AIDS 95, 99
Albemarle Report 113
Altruism 132
Assertiveness training 48
Association of Metropolitan Authorities (AMA) 90
Audit Commission 87

Basic education 84
Black Papers 139
Bolton General Hospital 85
'Butskellism' 30

Cambridgeshire village colleges 2, 17, 22, 29
Centralization of educational control 24, 54
Charity 132, 137
Charlie's Angels 136
'Charter 88' 134
Chartism 12
Children's rights 45
Christian perspective 118–29
Citizenship 3, 50, 93, 105–6, 128, 130–43, 146
City Technology Colleges 22
'Clause 28' 95, 99
Community
    as a concept 3, 29
    culture 109, 125
    and curriculum 64
    development 2, 40, 82, 87–93
    dialogical 116
    ideology of 20
Community associations 112
Community care 77, 78, 82–7
Community councils 39, 40
Community schools 19–22, 25, 26, 37
Conscientization 68
Consultation, of electorate by councils 90, 109–10
Continuing education 84
Councils, services provision by 88–93; see also Local education authorities
Countesthorpe College 18
Crucible Theatre, Sheffield 95, 99
Customer care 38, 87–93
Customers 31, 53, 90–2, 137

Democracy 13, 28, 148
    local 90
    participatory 140
    representative 132
'Dependency culture' 30
Dissidence 131, 139–43
Dual use of schools 42

Economic crisis 46
Economic inequality 2
Economic stagnation 127
Educare 120
Education Acts
    1870 12
    1902 (Balfour) 23
    1944 (Butler) 22, 23, 30, 57
    1986 22, 32, 37, 39, 45, 47, 53
Education Reform Act 1988 (Baker) 22–6, 32, 37, 39, 45, 47, 52, 53, 58, 122, 123, 127, 129
Educational Priority Areas 2
Educational standards 136

Electoral Reform Act 1928 14
Employment 69
Empowerment 6, 23, 25, 39, 68, 76, 94
Enterprise culture 24–6, 32, 70–1, 134
Equal opportunities 56–64, 90
European Commission 137

Facilitators 112
Feminism 9–15, 64, 94; see also Women's movement
Freedom 57, 132
    of choice 52
Fundamentalism 134
Fund-raising 42

Gender 99
Germany 130
Gingerbread 137
'Good life', the 132, 138
Greenham Common peace camp 96
Griffiths Report 78, 79
Guide movement 110

Hegemony 28, 30, 32
Historical roots of community education 10–15, 17–18, 20–2
Home–school relations 44
Homophobia 63, 146
Homosexuals 62–3, 96; see also 'Clause 28'

Immigration 58
Imperialism 145
Indoctrination 120, 141

Japan 130

'Kingdom', the, Christian concept of 121–2, 126

Lancashire Polytechnic 61
Learning Exchange 74
Left-wing politics, divisions in 134
Leicestershire Community College 2
'Liberal' and 'liberating' approaches to adult education, distinction between 10, 68–9
Life-long learning 25, 29, 38
Literacy 79, 81, 101
Liverpool Polytechnic 61, 82
Local education authorities
    diminishing role 31–2
    Rochdale, strategies followed by 37–43
Local Government and Housing Act 1988 89, 95
Lunacy Acts 1890, 1891 81

Market
    competition in the 31
    empowerment through the 49
    internal 30
Mechanics' institutes 11
Mental handicap 81
Mental illness 79, 81–5
Mental Treatment Act 1930 91
Mutual aid 112–15

'Nanny state' 30
National Advisory Body 59
National Council for Vocational Qualifications (NCVQ) 59
National Curriculum 22, 23, 39, 122, 127, 128, 135, 146
National Health Service 77, 137
Newcastle, local government in 89, 100
Newcastle Polytechnic 63
National Volunteer Force 136

151